W9-BZX-491

Children's poetry by X. J. Kennedy

KNOCK AT A STAR

KNOCK AT A STAR

A CHILD'S INTRODUCTION TO POETRY

X. J. KENNEDY
DOROTHY M. KENNEDY

Illustrated by Karen Ann Weinhaus

LITTLE, BROWN AND COMPANY

BOSTON   TORONTO

Illustrations copyright © 1982 by Karen Ann Weinhaus
Text copyright © 1982 by X. J. Kennedy and Dorothy M. Kennedy
All rights reserved. No part of this book may be reproduced in any
form or by any electronic or mechanical means including informa-
tion storage and retrieval systems without permission in writing
from the publisher, except by a reviewer who may quote brief
passages in a review.

Republished 1985

Library of Congress Cataloging in Publication Data

Main entry under title:

Knock at a star.

Includes indexes.
Summary: An anthology of mostly very short poems by stan-
dard, contemporary, and anonymous poets, intended to stimulate
interest in reading and writing poetry.
1. Children's poetry, American. 2. Children's
poetry, English. [1. American poetry—Collections.
2. English poetry—Collections] I. Kennedy, X. J.
II. Kennedy, Dorothy M. (Dorothy Mintzlaff) III. Weinhaus, Karen Ann, ill.
PS593.C45K6 1982   811'.008'09282   82–7328
ISBN 0–316–48853–4   AACR2
ISBN 0–316–48854–2 (pbk)

Acknowledgments appear on page 146.

BP

Published simultaneously in Canada
by Little, Brown & Company (Canada) Limited

Printed in the United States of America

CONTENTS

Contents

3   SPECIAL KINDS OF POETRY

Contents

1   WHAT DO POEMS DO?

MAKE YOU LAUGH

TELL STORIES

SEND MESSAGES

SHARE FEELINGS

START YOU WONDERING

MAKE YOU LAUGH

Poets, when they write nonsense, can turn our everyday world inside out and stand it on its ear.

Some poems are just for fun.

For instance...

The Ceiling

Suppose the Ceiling went Outside
And then caught Cold and Up and Died?
The only Thing we'd have for Proof
That he was Gone, would be the Roof;
I think it would be Most Revealing
To find out how the Ceiling's Feeling.

Theodore Roethke

On Learning to Adjust to Things

Baxter Bickerbone of Burlington
Used to be sheriff till he lost his gun.
Used to be a teacher till he lost his school.
Used to be an iceman till he lost his cool.
Used to be a husband till he lost his wife.
Used to be alive—till he lost his life.
When he got to heaven Baxter said,
"The climate's very healthy once you're used to being dead."

John Ciardi

Said Dorothy Hughes to Helen Hocking

Said Dorothy Hughes to Helen Hocking,
"I can't for the life of me get on this stocking!"
"Would it help if you first removed your shoes?"
Said Helen Hocking to Dorothy Hughes.

William Jay Smith

The Termite

Some primal termite knocked on wood
And tasted it, and found it good,
And that is why your Cousin May
Fell through the parlor floor today.

Ogden Nash

Algy

Algy met a bear,
The bear met Algy.
The bear was bulgy,
The bulge was Algy.

Anonymous

Who is Anonymous, anyway? Anonymous means "no name." In this book, we'll give this by-line to any poet whose name nobody knows. Anonymous, after Shakespeare, may be the second best poet in our language. At least, he and she wrote more good poems than most poets who sign what they write.

Song of the Pop-bottlers

Pop bottles pop-bottles
  In pop shops;
The pop-bottles Pop bottles
  Poor Pop drops.

When Pop drops pop-bottles,
  Pop-bottles plop!
Pop-bottle-tops topple!
  Pop mops slop!

Stop! Pop'll drop bottle!
  Stop, Pop, stop!
When Pop bottles pop-bottles,
  Pop-bottles pop!

Morris Bishop

The Great Auk's Ghost

The Great Auk's ghost rose on one leg,
Sighed thrice and three times winked
And turned and poached a phantom egg
And muttered, "I'm extinct."

Ralph Hodgson

There Was a Man

There was a man who never was.
This tragedy occurred because
His parents, being none too smart,
Were born two hundred years apart.

Dennis Lee

A Little More Cider

Miss Dinah when she goes to church,
She looks so neat and gay,
She has to take the dogs along
To keep the boys away.

A little more cider!
And a little more cider too!
A little more cider for Miss Dinah
And we all want some too!

Miss Dinah is a coffee pot,
Her skinny nose is the spout
And every time she stands on her head
She pours hot coffee out.

I went down to Miss Dinah's house
To fetch a side of beef.
She gave me a johnnycake to eat
So hard I broke two teeth.

Miss Dinah when she goes to bed
She gets all turned about.
She tucks the candle into bed
And blows her neck right out.

> *Anonymous*
> (American song, about 1845)

Knitted Things

There was a witch who knitted things:
Elephants and playground swings.
She knitted rain,
She knitted night,
But nothing really came out right.
The elephants had just one tusk
And night looked more
Like dawn or dusk.
The rain was snow
And when she tried
To knit an egg
It came out fried.
She knitted birds
With buttonholes
And twenty rubber butter rolls.
She knitted blue angora trees.
She purl stitched countless purple fleas.
She knitted a palace in need of a darn.
She knitted a battle and ran out of yarn.
She drew out a strand
Of her gleaming, green hair
And knitted a lawn
Till she just wasn't there.

Karla Kuskin

TELL STORIES

When you watch a superhero trashing a monster on TV, you're enjoying a kind of storytelling that began very long ago. The oldest long story in the western half of the world is *The Odyssey,* written in Greek. Its superhero tangles with a one-eyed giant, a witch who turns men into pigs, and other menaces. Nowadays, we think of stories as things found only in books, but in fact, until a few hundred years ago, most stories were poetry. People who couldn't read heard their stories from storytellers who would sing or chant or recite from memory.

The Odyssey is not only old, but long: more than fifteen thousand lines. Later, around the thirteenth century in England, short story songs called ballads became popular. Most are about lovers who die sadly, ghosts who return from the grave, heroes, such as Robin Hood, and other interesting people. Ballads are still being sung, and some have been written in America. Other kinds of story poems are still being written, too. Lately, some have been *very* short, like this:

Not Me

The Slithergadee has crawled out of the sea.
He may catch all the others, but he won't catch me.
No you won't catch me, old Slithergadee,
You may catch all the others, but you wo—

Shel Silverstein

Today, as in ancient times, poets like to spin good yarns. And still, some of the best poets tell of magic and marvels.

The Knowledgeable Child

I always see,—I don't know why,—
If any person's going to die.

That's why nobody talks to me.
There was a man who came to tea,

And when I saw that he would die
I went to him and said "Good-bye,

"I shall not see you any more."
He died that evening. Then, next door,

They had a little girl: she died
Nearly as quick, and Mummy cried

And cried; and ever since that day
She's made me promise not to say.

But folks are still afraid of me,
And, where they've children, nobody

Will let me next or nigh to them
For fear I'll say good-bye to them.

L. A. G. Strong

Travelers

The little girl was traveling unattached, as they say,
Closed into the window-seat by a heavy
Businessman working on papers out of his briefcase.
From across the aisle another kept noticing
What help she needed, her travel-case latched,
Her doll righted, coloring-book straightened out,
And he kept leaning over across to assist her.
After a while the heavyset man put away his papers,
Took out a small gameboard from his briefcase, and
  suggested,
How about a game of three-way parcheesi?

Josephine Miles

Incident

Once riding in old Baltimore,
  Heart-filled, head-filled with glee,
I saw a Baltimorean
  Keep looking straight at me.

Now I was eight and very small,
  And he was no whit bigger,
And so I smiled, but he poked out
  His tongue, and called me, "Nigger."

I saw the whole of Baltimore
  From May until December;
Of all the things that happened there
  That's all that I remember.

Countee Cullen

The White Stallion

(The Runaway)

A white horse came to our farm once
Leaping like dawn the backyard fence.
In dreams I heard his shadow fall
Across my bed. A miracle,
I woke beneath his mane's surprise;
I saw my face within his eyes,
The dew ran down his nose and fell
Upon the bleeding window quince....

But long before I broke the spell
My father's curses sped him on,
Four flashing hooves that bruised the lawn.
And as I stumbled into dawn
I saw him scorn a final hedge,
I heard his pride upon the bridge,
Then through the wakened yard I went
To read the rage the stallion spent.

Guy Owen

What Has Happened to Lulu?

What has happened to Lulu, mother?
  What has happened to Lu?
There's nothing in her bed but an old rag doll
  And by its side a shoe.

Why is her window wide, mother,
  The curtain flapping free,
And only a circle on the dusty shelf
  Where her money-box used to be?

Why do you turn your head, mother,
  And why do the tear-drops fall?
And why do you crumple that note on the fire
  And say it is nothing at all?

I woke to voices late last night,
  I heard an engine roar.
Why do you tell me the things I heard
  Were a dream and nothing more?

I heard somebody cry, mother,
  In anger or in pain,
But now I ask you why, mother,
  You say it was a gust of rain.

Why do you wander about as though
  You don't know what to do?
What has happened to Lulu, mother?
  What has happened to Lu?

Charles Causley

The Purist

I give you now Professor Twist,
A conscientious scientist.
Trustees exclaimed, "He never bungles!"
And sent him off to distant jungles.
Camped on a tropic riverside,
One day he missed his loving bride.
She had, the guide informed him later,
Been eaten by an alligator.
Professor Twist could not but smile.
"You mean," he said, "a crocodile."

Ogden Nash

Can a man work faster than a powerful machine? Such a man is remembered in a famous storytelling song. No, not Superman. John Henry.

Scholars believe John Henry really lived, although the song draws him larger than life. A black working man, he helped to build a railroad tunnel a mile and a quarter long. It went through a mountain near Hinton, West Virginia.

John Henry was a steel-driver, no doubt the greatest the Chesapeake and Ohio Railroad ever had. A steel-driver was the man who hammered a drill into a sheet of rock, making a hole to plant explosives in. His helper, the "shaker," held the drill, giving it a twist by hand after each blow of the steel-driver's hammer. That was hard, back-breaking work, and when a machine was invented to do the job, John Henry's "captain," or boss tunnel-builder, wanted to give it a try. So he set John Henry and the steam drill to work side by side, racing each other.

How the contest turned out has been sung, in different versions, for more than a hundred years.

John Henry

When John Henry was a little tiny baby
Sitting on his mama's knee,
He picked up a hammer and a little piece of steel
Saying, "Hammer's going to be the death of me, Lord, Lord,
  Hammer's going to be the death of me."

John Henry was a man just six feet high,
Nearly two feet and a half across his breast.
He'd hammer with a nine-pound hammer all day
And never get tired and want to rest, Lord, Lord,
  And never get tired and want to rest.

John Henry went up on the mountain
And he looked one eye straight up its side.
The mountain was so tall and John Henry was so small,
He laid down his hammer and he cried, "Lord, Lord,"
    He laid down his hammer and he cried.

John Henry said to his captain,
"Captain, you go to town,
Bring me back a TWELVE-pound hammer, please,
And I'll beat that steam drill down, Lord, Lord,
    I'll beat that steam drill down."

The captain said to John Henry,
"I believe this mountain's sinking in."
But John Henry said, "Captain, just you stand aside—
It's nothing but my hammer catching wind, Lord, Lord,
    It's nothing but my hammer catching wind."

John Henry said to his shaker,
"Shaker, boy, you better start to pray,
'Cause if my TWELVE-pound hammer miss that little piece
    of steel,
Tomorrow'll be your burying day, Lord, Lord,
    Tomorrow'll be your burying day."

John Henry said to his captain,
"A man is nothing but a man,
But before I let your steam drill beat me down,
I'd die with this hammer in my hand, Lord, Lord,
    I'd die with this hammer in my hand."

The man that invented the steam drill,
He figured he was mighty high and fine,
But John Henry sunk the steel down fourteen feet
While the steam drill only made nine, Lord, Lord,
    The steam drill only made nine.

John Henry hammered on the right-hand side,
Steam drill kept driving on the left.
John Henry beat that steam drill down,
But he hammered his poor heart to death, Lord, Lord,
   He hammered his poor heart to death.

Well, they carried John Henry down the tunnel
And they laid his body in the sand.
Now every woman riding on a C and O train
Says, "There lies my steel-driving man, Lord, Lord,
   There lies my steel-driving man."

Anonymous

Her strong enchantments failing

Her strong enchantments failing,
   Her towers of fear in wreck,
Her limbecks dried of poisons
   And the knife at her neck,

The Queen of air and darkness
   Begins to shrill and cry,
"O young man, O my slayer,
   Tomorrow you shall die."

O Queen of air and darkness,
   I think 'tis truth you say,
And I shall die tomorrow;
   But you will die today.

A. E. Housman

If you like to draw comics, here's an idea. Take the poem "Her strong enchantments failing" and make it into a comic strip with people saying the speeches in it. How will you make the young man look? The Queen of Air and Darkness?

A Story That Could Be True

If you were exchanged in the cradle and
your real mother died
without ever telling the story
then no one knows your name,
and somewhere in the world
your father is lost and needs you
but you are far away.

He can never find
how true you are, how ready.
When the great wind comes
and the robberies of the rain
you stand on the corner shivering.
The people who go by—
you wonder at their calm.

They miss the whisper that runs
any day in your mind,
"Who are you really, wanderer?"—
and the answer you have to give
no matter how dark and cold
the world around you is:
"Maybe I'm a king."

William Stafford

SEND MESSAGES

Poems often have a point to make. They leave us something to think about, and, like telegrams, they don't waste words.

Before Starting

A burro once, sent by express,
His shipping ticket on his bridle,
Ate up his name and his address,
And in some warehouse, standing idle,
He waited till he like to died.
The moral hardly needs the showing:
Don't keep things locked up deep inside—
Say who you are and where you're going.

Walker Gibson

Subway Rush Hour

Mingled
breath and smell
so close
mingled
black and white
so near
no room for fear.

Langston Hughes

Good Sportsmanship

Good sportsmanship we hail, we sing,
  It's always pleasant when you spot it.
There's only one unhappy thing:
  You have to lose to prove you've got it.

Richard Armour

Wanting

As a rule,
Man is a fool.
When it's hot
He wants it cool.
When it's cool
He wants it hot,
Always wanting
What is not.

Anonymous

This poem was first printed in 1917, before laws prevented children from working in factories.

The Golf Links

The golf links lie so near the mill
That almost every day
The laboring children can look out
And see the men at play.

Sarah N. Cleghorn

Spectacular

Listen,
a bird is singing.
Look,
up there!
He's on the rooftop
clinging
to the TV aerial,
singing
on prime time—
and no sponsor!

Lilian Moore

Childhood

I used to think that grown-up people chose
To have stiff backs and wrinkles round their nose,
And veins like small fat snakes on either hand,
On purpose to be grand.
Till through the banisters I watched one day
My great-aunt Etty's friend who was going away,
And how her onyx beads had come unstrung.
I saw her grope to find them as they rolled;
And then I knew that she was helplessly old,
As I was helplessly young.

Frances Cornford

Poor

I heard of poor.
It means hungry, no food,
No shoes, no place to live.
Nothing good.

It means winter nights
And being cold.
It is lonely, alone,
Feeling old.

Poor is a tired face.
Poor is thin.
Poor is standing outside
Looking in.

Myra Cohn Livingston

"Think as I think," said a man

❧❧

"Think as I think," said a man,
"Or you are abominably wicked;
You are a toad."

And after I had thought of it,
I said, "I will, then, be a toad."

Stephen Crane

Raccoon

The raccoon wears a black mask,
And he washes everything
Before he eats it. If you
Give him a cube of sugar,
He'll wash it away and weep.
Some of life's sweetest pleasures
Can be enjoyed only if
You don't mind a little dirt.
Here a false face won't help you.

Kenneth Rexroth

Landscape

What will you find at the edge of the world?
A footprint,
a feather,
desert sand swirled?
A tree of ice,
a rain of stars,
or a junkyard of cars?

What will there be at the rim of the earth?
A mollusc,
a mammal,
a new creature's birth?
Eternal sunrise,
immortal sleep,
or cars piled up in a rusty heap?

Eve Merriam

Dreams

Here we are all, by day; by night we are hurled
By dreams, each one into a several world.

Robert Herrick

A word is dead

A word is dead
When it is said,
Some say.
I say it just
Begins to live
That day.

Emily Dickinson

SHARE FEELINGS

How do you feel when you see a rainbow after a storm?
Are you surprised? Happy? Relieved that the storm is over?
William Wordsworth begins a poem by telling us how *he*
feels:

> My heart leaps up when I behold
> A rainbow in the sky.

Maybe the poet says what you feel about rainbows but
haven't been able to say. Or maybe rainbows don't usually
make you feel anything special at all. By sharing with you his
wonder and joy, the poet invites you—when next you see a
rainbow—to feel a special way about it, too.

Short poems that share feelings are called "lyrics." The
word *lyric,* by the way, comes from *lyre*—a stringed
instrument that in ancient Greece made music to go with
words, either sung or spoken. (That's why the words to
songs are also called lyrics today.)

Poetry can express many different moods: happiness,
sadness, anger, fear, loneliness. What feelings do you find in
these lyric poems?

And Stands There Sighing

Down from the north on the north wind flying
the wild geese come: I hear their crying.
Run to the door, and do not mind
that when they are gone, you'll be left behind.
For whoever hears the great flocks crying
longs to be off, and stands there, sighing.

Elizabeth Coatsworth

27

Christmas morning i

Christmas morning i
got up before the others and
ran
naked across the plank
floor into the front
room to see grandmama
sewing a new
button on my last year
ragdoll.

Carol Freeman

Hide and Seek

The trees are tall, but the moon small,
My legs feel rather weak,
For Avis, Mavis and Tom Clarke
Are hiding somewhere in the dark
And it's my turn to seek.

Suppose they lay a trap and play
A trick to frighten me?
Suppose they plan to disappear
And leave me here, half-dead with fear,
Groping from tree to tree?

Alone, alone, all on my own
And then perhaps to find
Not Avis, Mavis and young Tom
But monsters to run shrieking from,
Mad monsters of no kind?

Robert Graves

Beyond Words

That row of icicles along the gutter
Feels like my armory of hate;
And you, you...you, you utter...
You wait!

Robert Frost

An Historic Moment

The man said,
after inventing poetry,
"WOW!"
and did a full somersault.

William J. Harris

Country School

The Apple Valley School has closed its books,
wiped off its blackboard, put away its chalk;
the valley children with their parents' looks
ride busses down the road their parents walked.

The Apple Valley School is full of bales,
and the bell was auctioned off a year ago.
Under the teeter-totter, spotted quail
have nested where the grass would never grow.

The well is dry where boys caught garter snakes
and chased the girls into their memories.
High on the hill, nobody climbs to shake
the few ripe apples from the broken tree.

Ted Kooser

in Just-

in Just-
spring   when the world is mud-
luscious the little
lame balloonman

whistles   far   and wee

and eddieandbill come
running from marbles and
piracies and it's
spring

when the world is puddle-wonderful

the queer
old balloonman whistles
far   and   wee
and bettyandisbel come dancing

from hop-scotch and jump-rope and

it's
spring
and
    the

        goat-footed

balloonMan   whistles
far
and
wee

E. E. Cummings

Crying

Crying only a little bit
is no use. You must cry
until your pillow is soaked!
Then you can get up and laugh.
Then you can jump in the shower
and splash-splash-splash!
Then you can throw open your window
and, "Ha ha! ha ha!"
And if people say, "Hey,
what's going on up there?"
"Ha ha!" sing back, "Happiness
was hiding in the last tear!
I wept it! Ha ha!"

Galway Kinnell

While I Slept

While I slept, while I slept and the night grew colder
She would come to my room, stepping softly
And draw a blanket about my shoulder
While I slept.

While I slept, while I slept in the dark, still heat
She would come to my bedside, stepping coolly
And smooth the twisted, troubled sheet
While I slept.

Now she sleeps, sleeps under quiet rain
While nights grow warm or nights grow colder.
And I wake, and sleep, and wake again
While she sleeps.

Robert Francis

Zimmer in Grade School

In grade school I wondered
Why I had been born
To wrestle in the ashy puddles,
With my square nose
Streaming mucus and blood,
My knuckles puffed from combat
And the old nun's ruler.
I feared everything: God,
Learning, and my schoolmates.
I could not count, spell, or read.
My report card proclaimed
These scarlet failures.
My parents wrang their loving hands.
My guardian angel wept constantly.

But I could never hide anything.
If I peed my pants in class
The puddle was always quickly evident,
My worst mistakes were at
The blackboard for Jesus and all
The saints to see.
                    Even now
When I hide behind elaborate masks
It is always known that I am Zimmer,
The one who does the messy papers
And fractures all his crayons,
Who spits upon the radiators
And sits all day in shame
Outside the office of the principal.

                              Paul Zimmer

START YOU WONDERING

Poets, like the rest of us, love magic and mystery. Sometimes they'll tell us of ghosts, werewolves, dragons, creatures from far-off worlds. At other times, they'll weave a different kind of magic. They may show us everyday, ordinary things, but show them in new ways. For instance, did you ever think that an old toy magnet could be wonderful?

Magnet

This small
Flat horseshoe
Is sold for
A toy: we are
Told that it
Will pick up pins
And it does, time
After time; later
It lies about,
Getting its red
Paint chipped, being
Offered pins less
Often, until at
Last we leave it
Alone: then
It leads its own
Life, trading
Secrets with
The North Pole,
Reading
Invisible messages
From the sun.

Valerie Worth

The Magical Mouse

I am the magical mouse
I don't eat cheese
I eat sunsets
And the tops of trees
I don't wear fur
I wear funnels
Of lost ships and the weather
That's under dead leaves

I am the magical mouse
I don't fear cats
Or woodsowls
I do as I please
Always
I don't eat crusts
I am the magical mouse
I eat
Little birds—and maidens

That taste like dust

Kenneth Patchen

Science Fiction

From my city bed in the dawn I see a raccoon
On my neighbor's roof.
He walks along in his wisdom in the gutter
And passes from view
On his way to his striped spaceship to take his disguise off
And return to Mars as himself, a Martian
Raccoon.

Reed Whittemore

Daniel Boone

1735–1820

When Daniel Boone goes by, at night,
The phantom deer arise
And all lost, wild America
Is burning in their eyes.

Stephen Vincent Benét

The White Horse

The youth walks up to the white horse, to put its halter on
and the horse looks at him in silence.
They are so silent they are in another world.

D. H. Lawrence

The lightning and thunder

The lightning and thunder,
  They go and they come;
But the stars and the stillness
  Are always at home.

George MacDonald

The Child on the Shore

Wind, wind, give me back my feather
Sea, sea, give me back my ring
Death, death, give me back my mother
  So that she can hear me sing.

Song, song, go and tell my daughter
Tell her that I wear the ring
Say I fly upon the feather
  Fallen from the falcon's wing.

Ursula K. LeGuin

The Bird of Night

A shadow is floating through the moonlight.
Its wings don't make a sound.
Its claws are long, its beak is bright.
Its eyes try all the corners of the night.

It calls and calls: all the air swells and heaves
And washes up and down like water.
The ear that listens to the owl believes
In death. The bat beneath the eaves,

The mouse beneath the stone are still as death.
The owl's air washes them like water.
The owl goes back and forth inside the night,
And the night holds its breath.

Randall Jarrell

To see a world

To see a world in a grain of sand
And a heaven in a wild flower,
Hold infinity in the palm of your hand
And eternity in an hour.

William Blake

A Boat

O beautiful
was the werewolf
in his evil forest.
We took him
to the carnival
and he started
   crying
when he saw
the Ferris wheel.
Electric
green and red tears
flowed down
his furry cheeks.
He looked
like a boat
out on the dark
water.

Richard Brautigan

2 WHAT'S INSIDE A POEM?

IMAGES
WORD MUSIC
BEATS THAT REPEAT
LIKENESSES

IMAGES

Most of us like to bite into a tart, juicy apple. We wrinkle our noses if we smell a fish lying on a beach. We enjoy the music of an orchestra, the sight of a bluejay hopping on the snow, the warmth and fuzziness of a velour shirt. We take in the world around us through our five senses: sight, hearing, smell, taste, touch.

Most noses respond to the smell of bread baking in the oven. You may know you like that aroma, but can you catch it in words? Poets are willing to try. They can't make you actually *smell* bread baking, but if they are skillful they come close.

When a poet tries to capture in words, then, how something looks, tastes, smells, feels, or sounds, those descriptions are called images. Images can even help us imagine heat or cold. When John Keats wants us to sense how cold it is on a bitter evening, he writes: "The hare limped trembling through the frozen grass"— a line that almost makes you want to go *brrrr-r-r!*

Child on Top of a Greenhouse

The wind billowing out the seat of my britches,
My feet crackling splinters of glass and dried putty,
The half-grown chrysanthemums staring up like accusers,
Up through the streaked glass, flashing with sunlight,
A few white clouds all rushing eastward,
A line of elms plunging and tossing like horses,
And everyone, everyone pointing up and shouting!

Theodore Roethke

My Fingers

My fingers are antennae.
Whatever they touch:
Bud, rose, apple,
Cellophane, crutch—
They race the feel
Into my brain,
Plant it there and
Begin again.
This is how I knew
Hot from cold
Before I was even
Two years old.
This is how I can tell,
Though years away,
That elephant hide
Feels leathery grey.
My brain never loses
A touch I bring:
Frail of an eggshell,
Pull of a string,
Beat of a pulse
That tells me life
Thumps in a person
But not in a knife.
Signs that say:
"Please do not touch,"
Disappoint me
Very much.

Mary O'Neill

September

The breezes taste
  Of apple peel.
The air is full
  Of smells to feel—

Ripe fruit, old footballs,
  Burning brush,
New books, erasers,
  Chalk, and such.

The bee, his hive
  Well-honeyed, hums,
And Mother cuts
  Chrysanthemums.

Like plates washed clean
  With suds, the days
Are polished with
  A morning haze.

John Updike

Surprise

I lift the toilet seat
  as if it were the nest of a bird
and I see cat tracks
  all around the edge of the bowl.

Richard Brautigan

Windy Nights

Rumbling in the chimneys,
  Rattling at the doors,
Round the roofs and round the roads
  The rude wind roars;
Raging through the darkness,
  Raving through the trees,
Racing off again across
  The great grey seas.

Rodney Bennett

The Hound

It's funny to look at a hurrying hound
Pursuing a scent that's attractive.
He gallops around
With his nose to the ground
And only the back of him active.

Kaye Starbird

Snowy Benches

Do parks get lonely
in winter, perhaps,
when benches have only
snow on their laps?

Aileen Fisher

Mr. Wells

On Sunday morning, then he comes
To church, and everybody smells
The blacking and the toilet soap
And camphor balls from Mr. Wells.

He wears his whiskers in a bunch,
And wears his glasses on his head.
I mustn't call him Old Man Wells—
No matter—that's what Father said.

And when the little blacking smells
And camphor balls and soap begin,
I do not have to look to know
That Mr. Wells is coming in.

Elizabeth Madox Roberts

Winter Moon

How thin and sharp is the moon tonight!
How thin and sharp and ghostly white
Is the slim curved crook of the moon tonight!

Langston Hughes

Peach

Touch it to your cheek and it's soft
as a velvet newborn mouse
who has to strive
to be alive.

Bite in. Runny
honey
blooms on your tongue—
as if you've bitten open
a whole hive.

Rose Rauter

Spruce Woods

It's so still
today that a
dipping bough means
a squirrel
has gone through

A. R. Ammons

The Runner

On a flat road runs the well-trained runner,
He is lean and sinewy with muscular legs,
He is thinly clothed, he leans forward as he runs,
With lightly closed fists and arms partially raised.

Walt Whitman

WORD MUSIC

You or I, standing on a sandy beach in winter, might observe, "The ocean is rough today." A poet, seeing the same waves, might say, as in fact John Updike did in "Winter Ocean":

> Many-maned scud-thumper, tub
> of male whales, maker of worn wood, shrub-
> ruster, sky-mocker, rave!
> portly pusher of waves, wind-slave.

Such a poem is full of word music, as you'll hear if you read it aloud. Good poets choose words with care. They are as much interested in the sound of a word as in its meaning.

In one poem Emily Dickinson calls bees "buccaneers of buzz." The description is an apt one because like pirates (buccaneers), bees roam around and steal something: juice from flowers. The "buzz" imitates their sound, besides.

Edgar Allan Poe uses sounds in much the same way when he talks about "...the silken, sad, uncertain rustling of each purple curtain...." All those *sssssss* sounds almost set up a rustling in our ears.

Some poems don't *imitate* sounds, but *repeat* sounds. In Poe's lines, for instance, you can hear *s* sounds repeated, and also *r* sounds repeated inside the words. It's easy to notice such repetition when it comes at the beginnings of words: "Peter Piper picked a peck of pickled peppers." This famous tongue-twister repeats the *p* not to sound like a pickle but just because such repetition is fun. We find similar repetition (called "alliteration") in familiar sayings: "green as grass," "dead as a doornail," "tried and true." Such sounds often make your lips and mouth work.

In fact, reading good poems out loud, as it's fun to do, you may find that the poems are pretty "chewy." Then you may share what the poet James Wright discovered about reading

great poetry in his one-line poem, "Saying Dante Aloud":
"You can feel the muscles and veins rippling in widening and
rising circles, like a bird in flight under your tongue."

The Skaters

Black swallows swooping or gliding
In a flurry of entangled loops and curves,
The skaters skim over the frozen river.
And the grinding click of their skates as they impinge
       upon the surface,
Is like the brushing together of thin wing-tips of
       silver.

John Gould Fletcher

Rain

Like a drummer's brush,
the rain hushes the surfaces of tin porches.

Emanuel diPasquale

Some poets, and most songwriters, love to rhyme. Words rhyme when they end in the same sounds: *spoon* and *baboon, murky* and *turkey.* Rhyming words help knit a poem together. Besides, they're interesting to hear. Sometimes, they playfully bring together things you wouldn't expect to find in the same company:

> Julius Caesar,
> That Roman geezer,
> Squashed his wife with a lemon-squeezer.

To rhyme long words that way—words of two or more syllables—tends to sound funny. Some rhymes are exact, other rhymes are looser. Here's the beginning of a poem by Josephine Miles that first gives us an exact rhyme, then an inexact one:

> Went into a shoestore to buy a pair of shoes,
> There was a shoe salesman humming the blues
> Under his breath; over his breath
> Floated a peppermint lifesaver, a little wreath.

As you can see from those last two lines, rhymes depend not on spelling, but on sound. *Breath* and *wreath* are different sounds, though they end in the same letters. A rhyme like that is called an off-rhyme, or a slant rhyme.

Poems don't have to rhyme. In fact, most poems written today don't rhyme at all. Rhyme is just one of the pleasures that poets, if they want to, can provide.

Rural Recreation

Out here in Ringoes
I'm hitting fungoes
in my backyard
a big backyard.
Wherever I go
my brother Bing goes
he likes to sit here
and play the bongos
while I hit fungoes
soft and hard
and so the spring goes
out here in Ringoes.

Lillian Morrison

(In case you're wondering, Ringoes is a town in New Jersey. To hit a fungo, toss a baseball into the air and smack it with your bat as it drops.)

Did you eever, iver, over?

Did you eever, iver, over
In your leef, life, loaf
See the deevel, divel, dovel
Kiss his weef, wife, woaf?

No, I neever, niver, nover
In my leef, life, loaf
Saw the deevel, divel, dovel
Kiss his weef, wife, woaf.

Anonymous

My Old Cat

My old cat is dead,
Who would butt me with his head.
He had the sleekest fur.
He had the blackest purr.
Always gentle with us
Was this black puss,
But when I found him today
Stiff and cold where he lay
His look was a lion's,
Full of rage, defiance:
Oh, he would not pretend
That what came was a friend
But met it in pure hate.
Well died, my old cat.

Hal Summers

When I was christened

When I was christened
they held me up
and poured some water
out of a cup.

The trouble was
it fell on me,
and I and water
don't agree.

A lot of christeners
stood and listened:
I let them know
that I was christened.

David McCord

Here's a poem that looks like a solid block of words, but it rhymes all the way through. Read it aloud and see!

Football

The Game was ended, and the noise at last had died away, and now they gathered up the boys where they in pieces lay. And one was hammered in the ground by many a jolt and jar; some fragments never have been found, they flew away so far. They found a stack of tawny hair, some fourteen cubits high; it was the half-back, lying there, where he had crawled to die. They placed the pieces on a door, and from the crimson field, that hero then they gently bore, like soldier on his shield. The surgeon toiled the livelong night above the gory wreck; he got the ribs adjusted right, the wishbone and the neck. He soldered on the ears and toes, and got the spine in place, and fixed a gutta-percha nose upon the mangled face. And then he washed his hands and said: "I'm glad that task is done!" The half-back raised his fractured head, and cried: "I call this fun!"

Walt Mason

Analysis of Baseball

It's about
the ball,
the bat,
and the mitt.
Ball hits
bat, or it
hits mitt.
Bat doesn't
hit ball, bat
meets it.
Ball bounces
off bat, flies
air, or thuds
ground (dud)
or it
fits mitt.

Bat waits
for ball
to mate.
Ball hates
to take bat's
bait. Ball
flirts, bat's
late, don't
keep the date.
Ball goes in
(thwack) to mitt,
and goes out
(thwack) back
to mitt.

Ball fits
mitt, but
not all
the time.
Sometimes
ball gets hit
(pow) when bat
meets it,
and sails
to a place
where mitt
has to quit
in disgrace.
That's about
the bases
loaded,
about 40,000
fans exploded.

It's about
the ball,
the bat,
the mitt,
the bases
and the fans.
It's done
on a diamond,
and for fun.
It's about
home, and it's
about run.

May Swenson

BEATS THAT REPEAT

Here comes the parade! Drums tap. Trombones slide. Feet tramp the pavement. Arms steadily shuttle to and fro. "That band," we say, "has *rhythm.*"

What's rhythm? It's what you get when something happens regularly, again and again and again. Watch a little kid swinging on a swing and you'll notice a *rhythm* as the board departs and returns, departs and returns. You can also *feel* a rhythm, if you'll try the swing yourself.

At the ocean, waves roll in—crash—draw back—roll in again. You *see* their rhythm and *hear* their rhythm. Swim in the surf and you'll *feel* their rhythm, too. Rhythms arise from anything always recurring. You can speak of the rhythm of the seasons, the rhythm of day and night.

Poems, too, have rhythms you can see, hear, and feel. To find this out for yourself, read this next poem silently. (The "We" are some teenage tough guys. The Golden Shovel is a pool room where they hang out.)

We Real Cool
The Pool Players.
Seven at the Golden Shovel.

We real cool. We
Left school. We

Lurk late. We
Strike straight. We

Sing sin. We
Thin gin. We

Jazz June. We
Die soon.

Gwendolyn Brooks

Every sentence in the poem is made of three short words. That gives us a three-beat rhythm: "We real cool. We left school. We lurk late..." It's like *wham wham wham. Wham wham wham. Wham wham wham.* Do you notice what else is repeated? Periods. There's a period in the same place in every line. That gives us another rhythm, one made of stops. (Rhythms in poems are made out of little silences, as well as out of *whams*.) Besides, the poet gives us still another rhythm in the series of *We*'s. There's one *We* at the end of every line (except the last). So the rhythm of the poem goes like this:

> *wham wham wham* (stop) *wham* (pause)
> *wham wham* (stop) *wham* (pause)
> *wham wham* (stop) *wham* (pause)

And so on.

What we called a *wham*, poets call a *stress*. A stress is that extra oomph you give a word, or part of a word: a little more loudness, or breath. Say *banana* and you put the stress on the middle syllable (ba NA na). Say *tangerine*, and you don't stress the middle syllable, you stress the first syllable and the last (TAN ger INE). Every word in "We Real Cool" takes a stress, which makes the rhythm of the poem very powerful. Poets like to arrange words so that the stresses will fall into a pattern, and so give us a rhythm, as in this nonsense poem:

The Ostrich Is a Silly Bird

The *ostrich is* a *silly bird*
  With *scarcely any mind.*
He *often runs* so *very fast,*
  He *leaves* him*self* be*hind.*

And *when* he *gets* there, *has* to *stand*
  And *hang* about till *night,*
With*out* a *blessed thing* to *do*
  Un*til* he *comes* in *sight.*

  Mary E. Wilkins Freeman

In the poem above, the syllables that you stress are printed in *italic* letters to help you notice the rhythm. In this poem, the stresses fall on every *second* syllable, making a rhythm almost as regular as the ticking of a clock.

Poems don't usually stay that regular for very long. If they did, they might grow boring. (Luckily, Freeman's poem is funny—and short.) Here's a poem with a different rhythm in it—a rhythm like the gallop of a horse.

Windy Nights

Whenever the *moon* and *stars* are *set,*
  Whenever the *wind* is *high,*
All night long in the *dark* and *wet,*
  A *man* goes *ri*ding *by.*
Late in the *night* when the *fires* are *out,*
Why does he *gal*lop and *gal*lop a*bout?*

Whenever the *trees* are *cry*ing a*loud,*
  And *ships* are *tossed* at *sea,*
By, on the *high*way, *low* and *loud,*
  By at the *gal*lop goes *he.*
By at the *gal*lop he *goes,* and *then*
By he comes *back* at the *gal*lop a*gain.*

Robert Louis Stevenson

What suggests hoofbeats? Not just the word *gallop*. It's the rhythm inside the poet's lines. Notice the syllables with no *whams* on them. They tend to come in pairs. That makes for a rocking, or bouncing, rhythm. Read the poem aloud and feel it again. In a good poem, the rhythm—whether regular or changing—goes along with what the poet is saying in it.

Windshield Wiper

fog smog   fog smog
tissue paper   tissue paper
clear the blear   clear the smear

fog more   fog more
splat splat   downpour
rubber scraper   rubber scraper
overshoes   macintosh
bumbershoot   muddle on
slosh through   slosh through

drying up   drying up
sky lighter   sky lighter
nearly clear   nearly clear
clearing clearing veer
clear here clear

Eve Merriam

I am Rose

I am Rose my eyes are blue
I am Rose and who are you?
I am Rose and when I sing
I am Rose like anything.

Gertrude Stein

Ancient History

I hope the old Romans
Had painful abdomens.

I hope that the Greeks
Had toothache for weeks.

I hope the Egyptians
Had chronic conniptions.

I hope that the Arabs
Were bitten by scarabs.

I hope that the Vandals
Had thorns in their sandals.

I hope that the Persians
Had gout in all versions.

I hope that the Medes
Were kicked by their steeds.

They started the fuss
And left it to us!

Arthur Guiterman

Night Journey

Now as the train bears west,
Its rhythm rocks the earth,
And from my Pullman berth
I stare into the night
While others take their rest.
Bridges of iron lace,
A suddenness of trees,
A lap of mountain mist
All cross my line of sight,
Then a bleak wasted place,
And a lake below my knees.
Full on my neck I feel
The straining at a curve;
My muscles move with steel,
I wake in every nerve.
I watch a beacon swing
From dark to blazing bright;
We thunder through ravines
And gullies washed with light.
Beyond the mountain pass
Mist deepens on the pane;
We rush into a rain
That rattles double glass.
Wheels shake the roadbed stone,
The pistons jerk and shove,
I stay up half the night
To see the land I love.

Theodore Roethke

Canis Major

The great Overdog.
That heavenly beast
With a star in one eye,
Gives a leap in the east.

He dances upright
All the way to the west
And never once drops
On his forefeet to rest.

I'm a poor underdog,
But tonight I will bark
With the great Overdog
That romps through the dark.

Robert Frost

Blackberry Sweet

Black girl black girl
lips as curved as cherries
full as grape bunches
sweet as blackberries

Black girl black girl
when you walk you are
magic as a rising bird
or a falling star

Black girl black girl
what's your spell to make
the heart in my breast
jump   stop   shake

Dudley Randall

A Hero in the Land of Dough

Another nickel in the slot
And you will hit the Lucky Dot—
Down will pour the Great Jack Pot.

Up the Avenue you'll go
A Hero in the Land of Dough—
Ticker tape will fall like snow.

You will be the lucky one
Lolling in the summer sun
Watching lucky horses run

Watching lucky numbers spin,
You will be the next to win—
Put another nickel in.

Robert Clairmont

Triolet Against Sisters

Sisters are always drying their hair.
  Locked into rooms, alone,
They pose at the mirror, shoulders bare,
Trying this way and that their hair,
Or fly importunate down the stair
  To answer a telephone.
Sisters are always drying their hair,
  Locked into rooms, alone.

Phyllis McGinley

LIKENESSES

Poets are always putting things together in ways you wouldn't expect. A dog and a thunderstorm don't usually go together. In fact, when thunder and lightning start to boom and flash, all the dogs we know run into the house. But read these lines from a poem:

> Thunder threatens
> Like a sound that rolls around and around
> In a mean dog's throat.

The poet, Martha Sherwood, surprises us. She shows us how a storm and a dog are a lot alike. They make a noise that threatens.

Sometimes poets don't bother with the word *like;* they just go ahead and call one thing another: "Life is just a bowl of cherries," or "Get away from those cookies, you pig!" Nobody thinks a cookie-muncher has a tail and oinks. It's just the greedy way he eats that's piglike.

What things are brought together in these poems? What likenesses do the poets reveal?

The Wind

The wind stood up, and gave a shout;
He whistled on his fingers, and

Kicked the withered leaves about,
And thumped the branches with his hand,

And said he'll kill, and kill, and kill;
And so he will! And so he will!

James Stephens

Splinter

The voice of the last cricket
across the first frost
is one kind of good-by.
It is so thin a splinter of singing.

Carl Sandburg

Listening to grownups quarreling,

standing in the hall against the
wall with my little brother, blown
like leaves against the wall by their
voices, my head like a pingpong ball
between the paddles of their anger:
I knew what it meant
to tremble like a leaf.

Cold with their wrath, I heard
the claws of the rain
pounce. Floods
poured through the city,
skies clapped over me,
and I was shaken, shaken
like a mouse
between their jaws.

Ruth Whitman

Some common words
contain likenesses...

DAISY comes from two Old English
words meaning *day's eye*. (As you
can hear, daisy and day's eye
still sound almost alike.)

SQUIRREL comes from
Greek and means
shadow-tail.

CIRRUS in Latin means *lock of
hair*—so CIRRUS CLOUDS
are the kind that look hairy
or fleecy.

Child Frightened by a Thunderstorm

Thunder has nested in the grass all night
and rumpled it, and with its outstretched wings
has crushed the peonies. Its beak was bright,
sharper than garden shears and, clattering,
it snipped bouquets of branches for its bed.
I could not sleep. The thunder's eyes were red.

Ted Kooser

The house-wreckers

✺〄✺

The house-wreckers have left the door and a staircase,
now leading to the empty room of night.

Charles Reznikoff

When Paul Bunyan Was Ill

When Paul Bunyan was ill
we sent
twelve long-stemmed sequoias.

Willie Reader

Surf

Waves want
to be wheels,
They jump for it
and fail
fall flat
like pole vaulters
and sprawl
arms outstretched
foam fingers
reaching.

Lillian Morrison

Wind and Silver

Greatly shining,
The Autumn moon floats in the thin sky;
And the fish-ponds shake their backs and
   flash their dragon scales
As she passes over them

Amy Lowell

Thumb

The odd, friendless boy raised by four aunts.

Philip Dacey

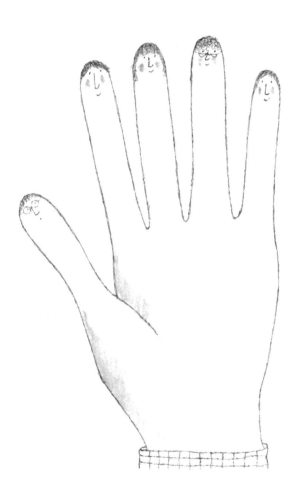

stars

in science today we learned
that stars are a mass of gases that burned
out a long time ago only we don't know
that because we still see the glow

and i remembered my big brother Donny
said he burned out a long time ago and i asked
him did that make him
a star

Nikki Giovanni

The Old Men Admiring Themselves
in the Water

I heard the old, old men say,
"Everything alters,
And one by one we drop away."
They had hands like claws, and their knees
Were twisted like the old thorn-trees
By the waters.
I heard the old, old men say,
"All that's beautiful drifts away
Like the waters."

William Butler Yeats

Epigram Engraved on the Collar of a Dog

Which I Gave to His Royal Highness

I am his Highness' dog at Kew;
Pray tell me, sir, whose dog are you?

Alexander Pope

3 SPECIAL KINDS OF POETRY

LIMERICKS

TAKEOFFS

SONGS

SHOW-AND-SPELL POEMS

FINDERS-KEEPERS POEMS

HAIKU

LIMERICKS

How the limerick began is uncertain. This kind of poem has the same name as a city in Ireland, but whether or not the first limericks came from Limerick, nobody knows. A limerick is a funny five-line poem in which the rhymes and rhythms are arranged like this:

> A bridge engineer, Mister Crumpett,
> Built a bridge for the good River Bumpett.
>   A mistake in the plan
>   Left a gap in the span,
> But he said, "Well, they'll just have to jump it."

Anonymous

The rhythm gallops. Long lines one, two, and five rhyme; so do shorter lines three and four.

Limericks started appearing in the early 1800s, but the form didn't become famous until Edward Lear wrote *The Book of Nonsense* in 1846. Here's one of his productions:

> There was a Young Person of Ayr,
> Whose Head was remarkably square:
>   On the top, in fine weather,
>   She wore a Gold Feather,
> Which dazzled the people of Ayr.

Usually, Lear repeated the first line in the last line that way.

The limerick has gone on to be the most popular kind of poem in the English language. At least, there are probably more limericks than any other kind. How come?

> Well, it's partly the shape of the thing
> That makes the old limerick swing—
>   Its accordion pleats
>   Full of light, airy beats
> Take it up like a kite on the wing!

Anonymous

There was an Old Man who said, "Hush!
I perceive a young bird in this bush!"
    When they said—"Is it small?"
    He replied—"Not at all!
It is four times as big as the bush!"

Edward Lear

There was an old person of Skye,
Who waltz'd with a Bluebottle fly:
They buzz'd a sweet tune,
To the light of the moon,
And entranced all the people of Skye.

Edward Lear

There was a young belle of old Natchez
Whose garments were always in patchez.
When comment arose
On the state of her clothes,
She drawled, When Ah itchez, Ah scratchez!

Ogden Nash

A piggish young person from Leeds
Made a meal on six packets of seeds
   But it soon came to pass
   That he broke out in grass
And he couldn't sit down for the weeds.

Anonymous

There was a young lady from Lynn
Who became so incredibly thin
   That in bringing her lip
   To some Coke for a sip
She slid down through the straw and fell in.

Anonymous

There was a young lady of Twickenham
Whose shoes were too tight to walk quick in 'em.
   She came back from her walk
   Looking white as a chalk
And took 'em both off and was sick in 'em.

Oliver Herford

Cried a man on the Salisbury Plain,
"Don't disturb me—I'm counting the rain;
   Should you cause me to stop
   I might miss half-a-drop
And would have to start over again."

Myra Cohn Livingston

There was an old man from Peru
Who dreamed he was eating his shoe.
   In the midst of the night
   He awoke in a fright
And—good grief! it was perfectly true!

Anonymous

There was an old lady named Crockett
Who went to put a plug in a socket;
   But her hands were so wet
   She flew up like a jet
And came roaring back down like a rocket!

William Jay Smith

Blesséd Lord, what it is to be young:
To be of, to be for, be among—
   Be enchanted, enthralled,
   Be the caller, the called,
The singer, the song, and the sung.

David McCord

TAKEOFFS

Sometimes it's fun, when you're singing a song or saying a poem, to make changes in it.

Just for the nonsense of it, you substitute a word or two of your own for a word or two of the poet's. So, "Mary had a little lamb" becomes *"Aladdin had a little lamp."* You're well on your way to writing a takeoff—also called a parody.

A favorite poem to take off from is "The Star" by Jane Taylor. It begins:

> Twinkle, twinkle, little star,
> How I wonder what you are
> Up above the world so high,
> Like a diamond in the sky.

Lewis Carroll, the author of *Alice in Wonderland,* made these playful changes in it:

> Twinkle, twinkle, little bat!
> How I wonder what you're at!
> Up above the world you fly,
> Like a tea tray in the sky.

Some writers of takeoffs don't merely change words. They will write a whole new poem from the beginning, as the first poet might have written it, only about something nutty.

Like somebody who dresses up in somebody else's clothes and does a little clowning, the writer of such a takeoff is borrowing the other poet's style. For instance, here's a famous poem in a simple style, easy to borrow:

This Is Just to Say

I have eaten
the plums
that were in
the icebox
and which
you were probably
saving
for breakfast

Forgive me
they were delicious
so sweet
and so cold

William Carlos Williams

Williams, by the way, was a doctor—a fact that Kenneth Koch remembers in writing these takeoffs:

Variations on a Theme by William Carlos Williams

1.
I chopped down the house that you had been saving to live
   in next summer.
I am sorry, but it was morning, and I had nothing to do
and its wooden beams were so inviting.

2.
We laughed at the hollyhocks together
and then I sprayed them with lye.
Forgive me. I simply do not know what I am doing.

3.

I gave away the money that you had been saving to live on
    for the next ten years.
The man who asked for it was shabby
and the firm March wind on the porch was so juicy and
    cold.

4.

Last evening we went dancing and I broke your leg.
Forgive me. I was clumsy, and
I wanted you here in the wards, where I am the doctor.

Kenneth Koch

Clementine

In a cavern, in a canyon,
    Excavating for a mine
Lived a miner, forty-niner,
    And his daughter, Clementine.

Oh, my darling, oh, my darling,
    Oh, my darling Clementine,
You are lost and gone forever,
    Dreadful sorry, Clementine.

Anonymous
(American popular song)

In a cavern, in a canyon

In a cavern, in a canyon
    Lay an unexpected mine.
Don't know where, Dear. DO TAKE CARE, DEAR...
    Dreadful sorry, Clementine.

Paul Dehn

Back Yard, July Night

Firefly, airplane, satellite, star—
How I wonder which you are.

William Cole

Sometimes, in writing a takeoff, a poet ends up writing a very different kind of poem. Eve Merriam, although she begins with a famous nursery rhyme, makes a not-so-funny point about city life....

Sing a Song of Subways

Sing a song of subways,
Never see the sun;
Four-and-twenty people
In room for one.

When the doors are opened—
Everybody run.

Eve Merriam

In 1772 Samuel Johnson wrote a takeoff on a poem he thought sounded stupid. (Almost nobody reads the original any more. It was "The Hermit of Warkworth" by Thomas Percy.) Dr. Johnson's takeoff is just four lines long:

I put my hat upon my head
And walk'd into the Strand;
And there I met another man
Whose hat was in his hand.

Nearly two hundred years later, the poet Donald Hall playfully added four more lines:

A Second Stanza for Dr. Johnson

I put my hat upon my head
And walk'd into the Strand;
And there I met another man
Whose hat was in his hand.

The only trouble with the man
Whom I had met was that,
As he walked swinging both his arms,
His head was in his hat.

Do you recognize the original for this takeoff? It has been sung by Scottish children on the streets of Edinburgh.

We four lads

We four lads from Liverpool are:
Paul in a taxi, John in a car,
George on a scooter, tootin' his hooter,
Following Ringo Starr!

Anonymous

SONGS

Here's a *very* old poem that people today still read. It is
written in the voice of some lonely person in England
wishing for the warm west wind to bring spring rain.

> Western wind, when wilt thou blow,
> That the small rain down can rain?
> Christ, if my love were in my arms
> And I in my bed again!

That poem began as a song, but no one remembers its
tune. Back when the poem was written, around 1500, most
poetry in English was still sung. It is only lately, since around
1620, that poets in general have stopped writing for singers
and musicians and have written mainly for readers. But there
are still poems to sing, both new and old.

Some popular songs you hear on the radio are poems, but
not all. If you just read their lyrics (the words without the
music) from a songsheet or a record jacket, sometimes the
words will seem silly, as flat and thin and forgettable as last
night's bathwater. There's no reason why a good song *has* to
be poetry, of course. You can sing any song and take pleasure
in it. But if its words contain vivid images and likenesses and
word music, then the song also gives you the special pleasure
of poetry.

You've already met some singable poems: "A Little More
Cider," "John Henry," "Clementine," and "We four lads."
Now here are other poems to sing. Some tell stories, some
(like "Western Wind") tell how the singer feels. One reward
in singing is that you may find yourself feeling the same way.
Maybe that's why everyone likes glad songs. But aren't there
times when a sad song—or a moody song—expresses just
what you need to feel?

Here's a favorite of recent folksingers. It's a modern
version of an English song over five hundred years old.

Riddle Song

G ... C ... G
"I gave my love a cher - ry that has no stone, I

D₇ ... G ... D₇
gave my love a chick - en that has no bone, I

D₇ ... G ... D₇
gave my love a gold ring that has no end, I

G ... C ... G D
gave my love a ba - by with no cry - in'."

2 How can there be a cherry that has no stone?
   How can there be a chicken that has no bone?
   How can there be a gold ring that has no end?
   How can there be a baby with no cry-in'?

3 A cherry when it's blooming, it has no stone.
   A chicken in the eggshell, it has no bone.
   A gold ring when it's rolling, it has no end.
   A baby when it's sleeping, has no cry-in'.

Anonymous

(Melody and guitar chords
transcribed by
John Jacob Niles)

On Top of Old Smoky

On top of old Smo-ky,——all co-vered with snow,——I
lost my true lov-er ——From court-in' too slow.——

2 Now, courtin's a pleasure,
   But parting is grief,
   And a false-hearted lover
   Is worse than a thief;

3 For a thief will just rob you
   And take what you have,
   But a false-hearted lover
   Will lead you to the grave;

4 And the grave will decay you,
   And turn you to dust.
   Not one boy in a hundred
   A poor girl can trust:

5 They'll hug you and kiss you,
   And tell you more lies
   Than the crossties on a railroad,
   Or stars in the skies.

6 So, come all you young maidens,
   And listen to me:
   Never place your affections
   In a green willow tree;

7 For the leaves they will wither,
   And the roots they will die.
   Your lover will forsake you,
   And you'll never know why.

                    Anonymous

93

Woodrow Wilson Guthrie, better known as Woody, was a poet, singer, and songwriter from Okemah, Oklahoma. He spent his young life in rambling the country, making friends and sometimes singing his songs for coins people threw into his hat. One of his many songs for (or about) children, "Turkey in the Corn" fits words to a tune popular with fiddlers, "Turkey in the Straw." Woody Guthrie said the words came to him "in the Army camp at Scott Field, Illinois, one hot summer's day looking over the fence at a big patch of green corn."

Turkey in the Corn

In a lit - tle bed a   wo - man was   born,   In a

lit - tle house a man was born, In a lit - tle time my ba - by was born to

run like a tur - key in my green June corn. Ri - ver come up and took my boards

Vine come up and took my gourds – Baby learned words from the winds and storm, to

run   like a tur - key in my green June corn.

2 The plow and hoe rung on my ground,
   Some days up and some days down,
   The sun and the moon went around and around
   And run like a turkey in my green June corn.
   My kitten it growed and my dog got bred,
   Old blind mare she feel down dead,
   Another little baby was born in my arm
   To run like a turkey in my green June corn.

Woody Guthrie

95

Catching free rides in railroad boxcars, traveling from place to place, sometimes working for a little money—that was the life of a hobo in America. One hobo dreamed of a wonderful land where everything he longed for grew on trees. Around 1900, he made up this famous song about it.

The Big Rock Candy Mountains

On a sum-mer's day in the month of May, A burly little bum come a hiking,
Trav-el-ing down that lone-some road A-look-ing for his lik-ing.

He was head-ed for a land that was far a-way, Be-side them cry-stal

foun-tains, 'I'll see you all this com-in' fall In the Big Rock Candy Mountains.'

STANZA 1

In the Big Rock Can-dy Moun-tains You nev-er change your socks, And

lit-tle streams of al-co-hol Come a-trick-l-ing down the rocks. The

box cars are all emp-ty And the rail-road bulls are blind, There's a lake of stew and

whis-ky, too, You can pad-dle all a-round' em in a big ca-noe In the

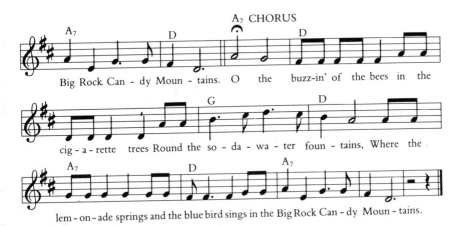

A₇ CHORUS

Big Rock Can - dy Moun - tains. O the buzz-in' of the bees in the cig - a - rette trees Round the so - da - wa - ter foun - tains, Where the lem - on - ade springs and the blue bird sings in the Big Rock Can - dy Moun - tains.

2 In the Big Rock Candy Mountains,
   There's a land that's fair and bright,
   Where the hand-outs grow on bushes
   And you sleep out every night,
   Where the box cars all are empty
   And the sun shines every day,
   O I'm bound to go, where there ain't no snow,
   Where the rain don't fall and the wind don't
      blow
   In the Big Rock Candy Mountains.

CHORUS: O—the buzzin' of the bees in the cigarette trees
         Round the soda-water fountain,
         Where the lemonade springs and the bluebird
            sings
         In the Big Rock Candy Mountains.

3 In the Big Rock Candy Mountains
   The jails are made of tin
   And you can bust right out again
   As soon as they put you in.
   The farmer's trees are full of fruit,
   The barns are full of hay.
   I'm going to stay where you sleep all day,
   Where they boiled in oil the inventor of toil
   In the Big Rock Candy Mountains.

   (CHORUS)

                    Anonymous

                    (Melody and guitar chords
                    transcribed by
                    Peggy Seeger)

97

We began with an ancient song about the wind. To end with, here's a modern one.

Blowin' in the Wind

2 How many times must a man look up
   before he can see the sky?
   Yes, 'n' How many ears must one man have
   before he can hear people cry?
   Yes, 'n' How many deaths will it take till he knows
   that too many people have died?
       The answer, my friend, is blowin' in the wind,
       The answer is blowin' in the wind.

3 How many years can a mountain exist
   before it's washed to the sea?
   Yes, 'n' How many years can some people exist
   before they're allowed to be free?
   Yes, 'n' How many times can a man turn his head
   pretending he just doesn't see?
       The answer, my friend, is blowin' in the wind,
       The answer is blowin' in the wind.
       The answer is blowin' in the wind.

Bob Dylan

SHOW-AND-SPELL POEMS

Good poetry is music to our ears. Sometimes, poems please our eyes as well.

The Dancing Bear

Slowly he turns himself round and round,
　　Lifting his paws with care,
Twisting his head in a sort of bow
　　To the people watching there.

His keeper, grinding a wheezy tune,
　　Jerks at the iron chain,
And the dusty, patient bear goes through
　　His solemn tricks again.

Only his eyes are still and fixed
　　In a wide, bewildered stare,
More like a child's lost in woods at night
　　Than the eyes of a big brown bear.

Rachel Field

Why does this poem look neat? Why is it three shapes in a stack? Because the poet wrote it in "stanzas," or clusters of lines joined with rhyme. On paper, Rachel Field has arranged her poem to show the rhyming lines. She indents them— that is, she pushes them in. And she leaves white space between the three stanzas.

Stanzas are the result of singing words to music. To prove this to yourself, try writing down the words of a song you know by heart, or have a recording of. End every line on a rhyme word. Group together each bunch of lines that rhyme together. You'll get stanzas. Now, "The Dancing Bear" isn't a song. Why is it in stanzas? In olden days most poems were sung. Stanzas are a habit that poets like Rachel Field have grown into.

Other poems may look more loosely scattered. They may be set on the page unevenly, like flowers in a vase:

The Innocent

The cat has his sport
and the mouse suffers
but the cat
    is innocent
  having no image of pain in him

    an angel
   dancing with his prey

carries it, frees it, leaps again
with joy upon his darling plaything

    a dance, a prayer!
how cruel the cat is to our guilty eyes

Denise Levertov

Here the poet may be trying to make certain words stand out. And if you read the poem aloud, pausing on the white spaces, those words may seem to matter all the more. Both poems, though very different, use words to say something *while arranging the words in eye-pleasing ways.*

One way a poet can please the eye is to place words into shapes, for the fun of it. Like this:

The Sidewalk Racer
Or, On the Skateboard

Skimming
an asphalt sea
I swerve, I curve, I
sway; I speed to whirring
sound an inch above the
ground; I'm the sailor
and the sail, I'm the
driver and the wheel
I'm the one and only
single engine
human auto
mobile

Lillian Morrison

The poem looks like what it's *about*. It's fun to see. (Being written with rhythm and rhyme, it's also fun to hear.)

In this next poem, Ian Hamilton Finlay is trying to show us not a solid object, but a motion. How well do you think he succeeds?

waterwheels in

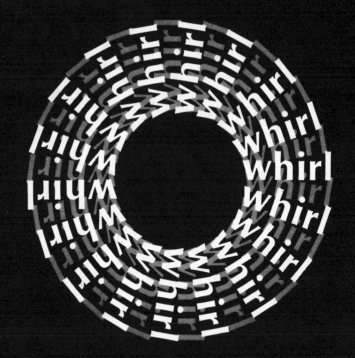

Fury said to a mouse

Fury said to
a mouse, That
he met
in the
house,
'Let us
both go
to law:
I will
prosecute
you. —
Come, I'll
take no
denial;
We must
have a
trial:
For
really
this
morning
I've
nothing
to do.'
Said the
mouse to
the cur,
'Such a
trial,
dear sir,
With no
jury or
judge,
would be
wasting
our breath.'
'I'll be
judge.
I'll be
jury,'
Said
cunning
old Fury;
'I'll try
the whole
cause,
and
condemn
you
to
death.

Lewis Carroll

grass path lasts

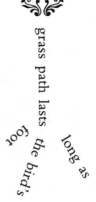

grass path lasts long as the bird's foot

Anita Virgil

Great frog race

GREAT
FROG
RACE

Ian Hamilton Finlay

For a Quick Exit

For going up or coming down,
in big department stores in town,
you take an escalator.
(They come in pairs.)
Or else an elevator.
(Also stairs.)

I wish storekeepers would provide

        a
         s
          l
           i
            d
             e
              !

Norma Farber

Concrete Cat

```
    A           A
  e   r       e   r

  eYe    eYe              stripestripestripestripe
whisker        whisker        stripestripestripe        t
            m   h  whisker  stripestripestripestripes      a   i   l   t   a   i   l
whisker    o   t  whisker      stripestripestripe
        U              stripestripestripestripe
                  stripestripestripestripe


      paw  paw        paw  paw              ǝsnoɯ

 dishdish                      litterbox
                               litterbox
```

Dorthi Charles

HANDSAWWWWWWWWWWWWWWWWWW

Richard Lebovitz

FINDERS-KEEPERS POEMS

Poetry is all around us, sometimes in words we hardly
bother to hear. We'll catch a striking phrase ("That new baby
is bright as a new penny") or an unusual name ("Spanish
Fork, Utah") or an old saying ("Red sky at night is the
sailor's delight," "The grass is always greener on the other
side of the fence"), and we'll realize with a start that we've
heard a bit of poetry. Once in a while you see some words,
not in a book, that don't claim to be poetry—and yet seem to
be. They say something that makes you think and feel about
it. There's something to remember in the very sound of the
words. Here's a sign that stands at the entrance to Great
Meadows National Wildlife Sanctuary in Concord,
Massachusetts:

> GATE
> UNLOCKS
> AT SUNRISE
> LIFT
> GENTLY
>
> TO OPEN

Nobody calls that sign a poem, but isn't it as good a poem as
many?

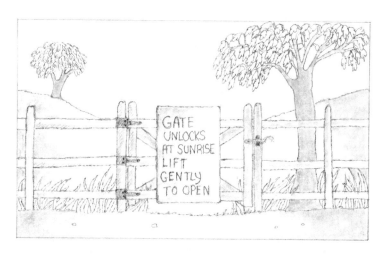

Lately some poets have been looking for poetry ready-made in the world around them, even in some places that don't seem promising: traffic signs, restaurant menus, recipes in cookbooks, labels on soup cans, billboards. Sometimes all the poet has to do is put the words into a new arrangement, as Ronald Gross does:

Yield

❧⟐❧

Yield.
No Parking.
Unlawful to Pass.
Wait for Green Light.
Yield.

Stop.
Narrow Bridge.
Merging Traffic Ahead.
Yield.

Yield.

You can see why such a poem is called a "found" poem. What did Gross make it out of? (Try reading it out loud, as if you're mad at somebody.)

See if you can figure out where the poets represented in this chapter "found" their poems.

Dorothy Wordsworth wrote these words in her journal. More than a century later, a scholar found them, liked them, arranged them in lines, and declared that Dorothy's brother William wasn't the only poet in the Wordsworth family.

The lake was covered all over

The lake was covered all over
With bright silverwaves
That were each
The twinkling of an eye.

Dorothy Wordsworth

Counting-out Rhyme

Grimes Golden Greening Yellow Transparent
York Imperial Wealthy Rome
McIntosh Milton Pippin Macoun
Stayman Winesap Courtland Newtown
Russet Baldwin Gravenstein
Ben Davis Jonathan Northern Spy
Delicious cider butter sauce or pie

Eve Merriam

To Become an Archer

To become an archer,
You should be for two
Years under a loom and not blink
Your eyes when the shuttle
Shoots back and forth:—

Then for three years
With your face turned
To the light, make a louse climb
Up a silk thread: When the
Louse appears to be

Larger than a wheel,
Than a mountain; when
It hides the sun: you may then
Shoot. You will hit it right
In the middle of the heart.

José Garcia Villa,
from Lao-Tse, quoted in
The Notebooks of Simone Weil, volume 1

4-Way Stop

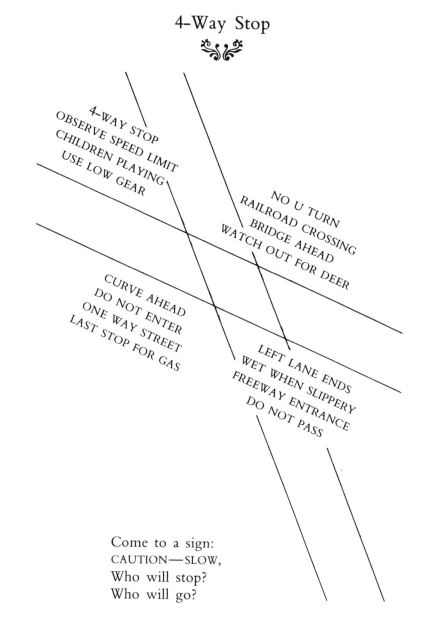

4-WAY STOP
OBSERVE SPEED LIMIT
CHILDREN PLAYING
USE LOW GEAR

NO U TURN
RAILROAD CROSSING
BRIDGE AHEAD
WATCH OUT FOR DEER

CURVE AHEAD
DO NOT ENTER
ONE WAY STREET
LAST STOP FOR GAS

LEFT LANE ENDS
WET WHEN SLIPPERY
FREEWAY ENTRANCE
DO NOT PASS

Come to a sign:
CAUTION—SLOW,
Who will stop?
Who will go?

Myra Cohn Livingston

Genuine Poem,
Found on a Blackboard
in a Bowling Alley
in Story City, Iowa

If you strike
when head pin
is red pin,
one free game
to each line.
Notify desk
before you throw
if head pin
is red

Ted Kooser

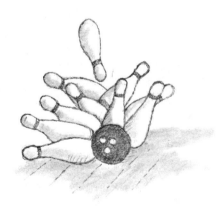

HAIKU

Haiku, which began in Japan, are short poems that keep you thinking and feeling for longer than they take to read. Because haiku may have started out as a game, the name means "beginning-verse." Players, given a haiku, were supposed to go on and make a longer poem out of it. But some haiku came to be well known, short as they are. Here are some Japanese haiku in translation:

Ancient pool. Sound
of a frog's leap—
Splissssshhhhh....

Bashō
(translated by Olivia Gray)

A bantam rooster
spreading his ruff of feathers
thinks he's a lion!

Kikaku
(translated by Harry Behn)

Small bird, forgive me.
I'll hear the end of your song
in some other world.

Anonymous
(translated by Harry Behn)

In Japanese, haiku are just seventeen syllables long. If you're writing a haiku in English, though, you don't have to keep exactly to that count. The main thing is to keep it short and, if possible, in three lines. Because the poem *is* so brief, you don't have room to talk about your inner feelings. You just point to something and let it make the reader (or listener) feel something, too. A good haiku, tossed out into your reader's mind, should go on and on—like the waves from the frog's leap into the pool.

Now the swing is still:
a suspended tire
    centers the autumn moon.

Nicholas Virgilio

About an excavation
a flock of bright red lanterns
has settled.

Charles Reznikoff

Coming from the woods
A bull has a lilac sprig
Dangling from a horn

Richard Wright

The green cockleburs
Caught in the thick wooly hair
Of the black boy's head

Richard Wright

sky
is towing the old man
on kite string

Raymond Roseliep

child
in a window:
knock at the moon

Raymond Roseliep

Deep in the rippling spring
an old rubber Popeye toy
blows bubbles.

May Ushida

After weeks of watching the roof leak
I fixed it tonight
by moving a single board.

Gary Snyder

One of the Years

Hat pulled low at work,
I saw the branding iron
Take the first snowflake.

William Stafford

Bang! the starter's gun—
    thin raindrops
      sprint.

Dorthi Charles

4 DO IT YOURSELF

(WRITING YOUR OWN POEMS)

DO IT YOURSELF

Maybe browsing among the poems in this book has inspired you to try some writing. Whether or not you are a gifted poet, you can have fun writing verse of your own. Find a quiet place to work; then be lazy and let your ideas play. You need very little equipment—just paper and a pencil or pen.

Watch a second grader building a castle with a set of wooden blocks. He piles up some big, smooth, cube-shaped ones and puts a cone or pyramid on top. He knocks them down and starts over. He finds just the right cylinder for a turret, and he tops that with a cone-shaped roof. He knocks down the bridge over the moat because he has found a bigger block that will make a stronger bridge. He is enjoying himself thoroughly.

In much the same way, a poet likes to build playfully with words. He may begin with a few good-sounding ones. He crosses them out and substitutes better ones. He moves a whole line from the top of the page to the bottom. He reads a line aloud and adds a word. He is having a fine old time. And, if he is a good poet, he ends up with a stronger poem than the one he began. Poems not only can be fun to write; they can be fun to improve.

There are, it is true, a few dangers to avoid as you start putting words down on paper. Say you have just read "A Vagabond Song" by Bliss Carman, which starts out:

> The scarlet of the maples can shake me like a cry
> Of bugles going by.

You might think, "That's beautiful! I want to write something just like it!" And then you may plunge into your own tribute to red leaves. But stop and think. Does the sight of leaves on a tree really and truly affect you deeply? If red

leaves don't make you feel much of anything, *don't pretend.*
Phony baloney = bad poetry.

A not-very-good poet once wrote:

> In the prison cell we sit—
> Are we broken-hearted? Nit!

In those lines, the rhyme is giving orders to the poet instead
of the other way around. Very likely, what the writer *wanted*
to say was:

> In the prison cell we sit—
> Are we broken-hearted? No!

—but he felt he had to force his poem to rhyme. If you face a
choice between rhyming and saying what you mean, it is a
whole lot better to say what you mean. With practice, you
can learn to do so and rhyme, too; but not all poems need to
rhyme, so don't feel that yours absolutely *has* to.

Poems don't have to be solemn and serious, either. A sense
of humor is as welcome in a poet as in anyone else.

If you'd like to write a poem, but don't know how to
begin, here are a few suggestions to help you get started.

IDEAS

1. Look around you for words. You can find them on traffic signs, cereal boxes, travel posters, in textbooks, newspaper stories, ads, and just about everywhere else. Select the most interesting of those words, try rearranging them in whatever order pleases you, and see if you can make a "found poem" like the ones on pages 108–113.

2. Reexamine the show-and-spell poems on pages 100–107. Try to write a shaped poem of your own. First pick a small object with a simple shape everybody can recognize: a star, a bird, a pyramid, an ice-cream cone. A large, complicated shape, such as a football team or a stegosaurus, might be pretty hard to build out of words. Then write a short poem about that object, not worrying yet about the shape. When you have your poem the way you want it, pencil the shape on a piece of paper and try writing or typing the words into it.

3. Maybe you are familiar with:

> Teddy bear, teddy bear, turn around,
> Teddy bear, teddy bear, touch the ground,
> Teddy bear, teddy bear, show your shoe,
> Teddy bear, teddy bear, out go you!

This and a lot of other jump-rope rhymes have been chanted by generations of jumpers. Can you write a new one? Don't forget to try it out on the playground!

To help you get started, here's a new jump-rope rhyme made up by William Jay Smith:

Brooklyn Bridge

Brooklyn Bridge, Brooklyn Bridge,
I walked to the middle, jumped over the
edge,

The water was greasy, the water was
brown
Like cold chop suey in Chinatown,

And I gobbled it up as I sank down, —
Down—
Down—
Down—
Down—

Brooklyn Bridge, Brooklyn Bridge,
I walked to the middle, looked over the
edge.

But I didn't jump off, what I said's
not true—
I just made it up so I could scare you:
Watch me jump!—
Watch me jump!—
Watch me jump!—
BOO!

4. Write a nonsense poem. Many young writers like to start with a limerick. You will find some good examples back on pages 78–83.
5. Write a takeoff on any poem you like. Or don't like.
6. Write a poem in which you try accurately to describe something: a person of your acquaintance, a place, or any object. Then see if a friend can recognize your subject, just by reading your poem. (If the friend can't, then try again.)
7. Write a poem that appeals to one of your five senses: taste,

smell, touch, sight, hearing. William Carlos Williams's poem can be your model if the sense of sight is your choice:

Poem

As the cat
climbed over
the top of

the jamcloset
first the right
forefoot

carefully
then the hind
stepped down

into the pit of
the empty
flowerpot

(See pages 42–49 for some poems calling up other senses.)

8. Have you had an experience, a thought, or a feeling you'd like to share? Write it into a poem.
9. After you've read the haiku on pages 114–118, try to write one of your own. Remember, it doesn't have to rhyme. Just try to keep it within three short lines. Start with something you've actually seen or heard or touched or smelled or tasted. A haiku doesn't have room to let you blab about your feelings. You can't say,

> Oh, poor me!
> Nobody likes me.
> How sad I am.

—or you'll use up all your space. Some haiku poets start with one image, then add another that acts together with the first:

> On the one-ton temple bell
> a butterfly, folded into sleep,
> sits still.

When these two oddly matched things meet (bell weighing a ton, frail butterfly), the effect on the reader is a little surprise. It is almost as though the heavy bell had rung.

Do It Yourself

Buy our little magazine
Quite the smallest ever seen
Printed on a square of tissue
Just
One
Letter
In
Each
Issue.
With each issue, given free
A seed pearl and a pinch of tea.

Thread the seed pearl, save the pinch,
Make a necklace, inch by inch,
Fill a warehouse, ton by ton,
Save the letters, one by one,
Lay
The
Letters
In
A
Row
Make the rhyme you're reading now

Joan Aiken

Whether you're a poet or not, you can have a fine time trying to write your own poetry. The effort, while it just might have you tearing your hair with frustration, should at least increase your respect for good poets and good poetry. If it does, then your writing will have led you to a valuable treasure indeed. After all, playing ball yourself is one way to learn to admire and enjoy the skill of big league ballplayers.

And—who knows? To have written a poem you want to keep may leave you joyful. You may even catch a glimmer of what Robert Herrick meant, when, more than three hundred and fifty years ago, he likened the joy of writing a poem to being crowned with roses. "I should delight," he prayed, to write another poem,

> *And once more yet (ere I am laid out dead)*
> *Knock at a star with my exalted head.*

AFTERWORD TO ADULTS

Lucky is the child whose nearest adults are themselves affectionate readers of poetry. More fortunate still is the child who from earliest years has listened to poems read or sung. By the time such children can read for themselves, they are already at home with poetry.

People who wish their children to grow up liking poetry do well, we believe, to start reading aloud to them as soon as they can sit up and help turn pages. Whether the text be Mother Goose or Dr. Seuss, there is nothing like a warm lap or an enclosing arm and a friendly voice to encourage a child to love words. More than mere fondness for poetry is at stake. We have no evidence, but we suspect that a close correlation may be drawn between reading skills and the use of a book instead of television as a bedtime comforter.

Because your own taste is likely to influence the child's, we suggest that you share with children only those poems you like. What bores you will probably bore them, too.

With or without an early start, most children, even those of eight or older, will immediately respond to vigorous, plainspoken poems. As William Stafford remarks of children (in his "Keepsakes"):

> They dance before they learn
> there is anything that isn't music.

Despite the glare of video screens, skipping ropes continue to twirl, filling the air not only with jumpers but with timeless jingles:

> Grace, Grace, dressed in lace,
> Went upstairs to powder her face.
> How many boxes did she use?
> One, two, three...

It is later, usually in secondary school, that distaste for poetry sets in, like frost. It tends to arrive when the child is assigned to write papers on poems, and comes to suspect from class discussions that the meaning of poetry is the secret, exclusive property of English teachers. Before that happens, caring adults may help children realize that poetry is fun—and revelation. (For those teachers, and fortunately they are legion, who treat poetry as a joy, we have included "A Note to People Who Wish to Use This Book in Working with Groups.")

Our book is directly addressed to children from eight to twelve, more or less: those who can read for themselves, and want to do so. The book may simply be placed in their hands so that they may decide for themselves whether to have any truck with it. To be sure, any encouragement or interest the giver can contribute will undoubtedly help. It would be great if the nineteenth-century custom of parents' reading aloud to children were to be reborn in present-day America. In a family of two or more children, a rewarding practice is to have an older child read poetry to a younger; in a one-child family, you can always enlist the babysitter. (The point is that the older child, or the sitter, may benefit as much as the audience.)

In this book we gather poems that, in our experience, have amused, delighted, and engaged children in third through sixth grade. We have tried to leave out what children "ought" to like. In some classic anthologies, unrealistic views of a child's attention span prevail. Some anthologists let in the more trivial and forgettable efforts of Shakespeare, Milton, and other giants, or represent them by little snippets. We have worked in the faith that, to a child, great names matter less than graspable poems. Several great names have got into this book, too, but they are attached to poems we think children will like. We suspect that poems children cannot at least partially understand aren't likely to stay with them. Our assumption is that children who learn to love poems—poems they can see eye to eye with—may well advance to poems of greater complexity.

Except for a couple of excerpts admitted to the section of "Takeoffs," we have generally limited our choices to whole poems originally written in English. Poetry in English seemed vast enough to represent in a short introduction, but an exception has been made in the book's section on haiku, a form best demonstrated with the aid of some translations from the Japanese.

Children turn aside from poets who talk down to them, as in the kind of sweet, confected poem (less often written these days than formerly) that seems to say, "Here, little man or woman, is a verbal lollipop for you." Poems that children like may take in any reality at all. Many of our selections state values—for instance, Stephen Crane's " 'Think as I think,' said a man," or "My Old Cat" by Hal Summers—but we have tried to leave out poems that moralize. In general, we sought poems whose language is direct and contemporary; poems that, however short, are laden to the brim. We looked for what seemed feelingful, vivid and concrete in imagery, rhythmic, rich in sound, and, whenever possible, graced with a little magic.

That children love to scrutinize things at close range persuades us that they may, with a little adult encouragement, care to look closely at poems as well. Inviting young readers to analyze poems, we are aware, flies in the face of much expert advice. A frequent assumption is that asking children to look closely at a poem may kill whatever pleasure they may take in it. Although we share the view that excessive analysis is dangerous, and that there is something wrong with (as Elizabeth Bishop once put it) "making poetry monstrous or boring and proceeding to talk the very life out of it," we believe just as strongly that the insides of a poem may interest children greatly. Children delight in learning the rules of games; and poetry, in its forms and measures, often has gamelike elements. For the child who likes to look closely at a living animal, insect, or plant, at a machine or a mineral specimen, a poem also rewards close attention. It invites readers to see how it works. We wouldn't be afraid to point out a few things we've noticed in a poem—even a rhythm or a rhyme scheme—or to invite kids to point out anything interesting they've noticed, too.

Neither do we accept the fashionable belief that every child is a born poet whose least utterance merits praise. Most poems written by children, like most poems by anybody, are chaff for the wind to drive away. Yet we have included a chapter on writing poems, for in feeling their way into poetry, children can learn much from trying to write poems. At least they will find that good poetry is hard to write, and so may relish all the more what poets have accomplished.

Any introduction to the Muse, of course, will leave some young readers feeling, "Ah, so what?" This need not discourage you, or us. Not all adults care for poetry, either; yet most manage to be useful citizens, even reasonably happy ones. Poetry cannot redeem the world, but it has undisputed rewards for those willing to receive them. It can, at least for a moment, heighten the experience of being alive. It can sharpen the wits, awaken the imagination, perhaps even leave a grain of wisdom behind. This seems enough to ask of it.

A NOTE TO PEOPLE WHO WISH TO USE THIS BOOK IN WORKING WITH GROUPS

For those teachers who wish to bring this book to class; for librarians who work with reading groups; for poets who visit schools; and for parents or other adults who wish to start a group of children reading poetry, here are a few suggestions.

Because good poems are made of well-chosen words, words worth paying attention to, there is nothing better than reading them aloud. Before reading to a group, however, an inexperienced adult had better practice. Every reader-aloud of poetry needs to understand what a poem is saying, and needs to share some of the poet's apparent feelings. A tape recorder, so you can hear yourself, may be helpful; and if children are encouraged to read aloud, too, they may enjoy hearing their own readings on tape. A temptation to avoid— and it is one into which groups of kids tend to fall, when given a metrical, regularly rhythmic poem—is to read in a singsong chant, which renders the poem monotonous and feelingless. Read with some oomph yourself: at least, whatever oomph you honestly feel. Don't be afraid to ham it up, within reason. Children aren't stern drama critics. (Incidentally, it may be worth pointing out sometimes that there are some poems *not* meant to be read aloud: puzzling or difficult poems that take slow figuring-out; visual poems, like those in the "Show-and-Spell" section of this book.)

In reading aloud, it helps if children and adults group themselves together: not in a theatrical situation with the adult up front as if on pulpit or podium, but with everybody relaxed, sitting elbow to elbow, in a circle on the floor or in any close arrangement that is comfortable. With children of eight or nine, about twenty minutes of poetry reading at a stretch is usually plenty. Even adult poetry audiences seldom can listen to poetry for more than fifty minutes. Children will quickly alert you when they are restless; they will probably want to get up and run around. So don't oversupply them with material, and intersperse moments of relaxation and physical exercise.

Fine recordings of poets reading their works are available: Robert Frost, Dylan Thomas, E.E. Cummings, and Edna St. Vincent Millay are among the celebrated readers. However, while kids may be asked to do a brief amount of such listening, we find that only teenagers are likely to listen to recordings patiently for very long. On the eight-to-twelve age level, poetry works best when the auditors are given a chance to take part. One method is choral reading, in which the group members all read from a copy of a poem displayed on a card or chalkboard or projected slide (a device that probably brings people together more than if each reads from an individual copy). Here again, care needs to be taken lest a choral reading become a monotonous singsong. Some experienced teachers have reported good luck in using a poem full of repetitions: a chorus or refrain that the kids can speak together, while a single voice (perhaps the adult's) reads the other lines of the stanzas.

Some people like to use songs that have definite beats, and ask the kids to clap to a rhythm. It's worth a try, but we admit we have never had much luck with it ourselves. The custom tends just to mess up the beat, as the clappers can't always agree on their timing. Anyhow, it is probably the meaning of the poem that needs stressing, not the regular beat, if any. The regular beat will make itself heard, but its effect is subtler than hand clapping. Those blessed with musical skills, who can bring in a guitar or a pair of castanets, can make kids memorably aware that many poems are songs.

Children may be invited to illustrate the poems they hear—a playful activity that focuses their visual imaginations onto paper. Although we have no powerful convictions about this, we suspect it is probably better if the drawings are kept to simple sketches. Poems do much more than enter pictures in our heads; good poems suggest, perhaps indefinitely.

Should children be asked to memorize poetry? Most of us over thirty, who have been exposed to required memorization in elementary school, are sometimes astonished to realize how clearly certain poems or documents (Lincoln's Gettysburg Address, the Preamble to the Constitution) stick in memory. Yet memorization is in the doghouse with many educators these days, perhaps because in the past teachers overworked it. Although we don't encourage children to commit long, incomprehensible passages to memory, our feeling is that the idea of memorization deserves a fresh look and has been, perhaps, too vigorously detested. Some children cannot memorize to save their necks, and shouldn't be expected to try; but we think it does no harm to ask a group—in the course of a happy and successful reading party—"Who can say that poem over again?" Or: "Who can say a poem out loud? Any poem you remember." (You may collect a few living specimens of contemporary childhood jingles!) So employed, memorization isn't a chore, but one more way of reminding children that poems aren't merely to be seen, but also to be heard, and kept.

Here are a few rules of thumb for those who invite children to write poetry:

1. Before having children write, have them read and hear good poems.
2. At first, ask for only brief poems, not more than six or eight lines.
3. Tell them that poems don't need to rhyme. But if their poems *want* to rhyme, let them.
4. In your suggestions for writing, offer choices. Your suggestions do not have to be a list of possible subjects to write about. Poems may begin from anything: not only a subject, but a word, a feeling, a thing seen.
5. Don't wax enthusiastic about mediocre stuff. Don't be afraid to offer a kind suggestion for improvement, or to wonder about a line you can't understand. Just don't smother the child with nit-picking technical advice.
6. Don't encourage the prolonged public tearing apart of poems produced. Ask not just for faultfinding; ask what parts of a poem listeners *like*.
7. If you have the children haul out pencils and write poems on the spot in five or ten minutes, do not expect the results to be wonderful. Some of the best poets are slow thinkers, and need to rewrite and rewrite. Urge children to keep working on their poems, with the understanding that they can show their finished versions to the group at a later time.
8. Do provide some form of publication for any poems you admire. A mimeographed one-sheet poetry magazine might inspire contributors, or even a display of poems thumbtacked to a bulletin board.

For reading and borrowing, an armful of poetry books of wildly different kinds is valuable artillery. Let the kids shuffle through them and make their own choices. For some bibliography, see Nancy Larrick, *A Parent's Guide to Children's Reading,* fourth edition (New York: Bantam Books, 1977); Zena Sutherland and May Hill Arbuthnot, *Children and Books,* fifth edition (Glenview, Illinois: Scott Foresman, 1977); Abby Campbell Hunt, *The World of Books for Children* (New York: Sovereign Books, 1979), and current issues of *The Horn Book* magazine.

One of the more formidable obstacles to children's borrowing of poetry from the library seems to be the Dewey Decimal System, which buries poetry off in the 800s, remote from where children look for recreational reading matter. All praise to the many librarians who occasionally outwit Dewey by bringing a sheaf of poetry books out of the 800s and displaying them on a special, more accessible lending shelf.

Working with groups of children, you never know what to expect, of course—and that is part of the joy of it. Above all, be modest in your expectations. Don't feel that every child is duty-bound to love poetry. Every child probably will, at the very least, stand for it. Most will enjoy some of it and, seeing that you care for poetry yourself, will want to share your pleasure in it.

INDEX OF AUTHORS

A page number in *italics* indicates a quotation.

INDEX OF TITLES

INDEX OF FIRST LINES

Acknowledgments

For permission to include copyrighted material, we gratefully make the following acknowledgments:

Addison-Wesley Publishing Company for four lines beginning "I am Rose," reprinted from *The World Is Round* by Gertrude Stein. Copyright 1939 by Gertrude Stein. Copyright renewed by Daniel C. Joseph, Admr. d.b.n. CTA of the Estate of Gertrude Stein. By permission of Addison-Wesley Publishing Company, Reading, MA.

George Allen & Unwin Ltd. for "The Great Auk's Ghost" from *The Last Blackbird* by Ralph Hodgson.

Atheneum Publishers, Inc. for "Cried a Man on the Salisbury Plain" from *A Lollygag of Limericks* by Myra Cohn Livingston. A Margaret K. McElderry Book (New York: Atheneum, 1978). Copyright © 1978 by Myra Cohn Livingston. For "Poor" from *The Way Things Are and Other Poems* by Myra Cohn Livingston. A Margaret K. McElderry Book (New York: Atheneum, 1974). Copyright © 1974 by Myra Cohn Livingston. For "Spectacular" from *I Thought I Heard the City* by Lilian Moore (New York: Atheneum, 1969). Copyright © 1969 by Lilian Moore. All selections reprinted by permission of Atheneum Publishers.

Alison Kingsbury Bishop for "Song of the Pop-Bottlers" from *The Best of Bishop* by Morris Bishop (Cornell University Press, 1980). Copyright 1950, © 1978. First appeared in *The New Yorker.*

John F. Blair, Publisher, and Dorothy Owen for "The White Stallion" from *The White Stallion* by Guy Owen (John F. Blair, Publisher, 1969).

Brandt & Brandt Literary Agents, Inc., for "Daniel Boone" by Stephen Vincent Benét from *A Book of Americans* by Rosemary and Stephen Vincent Benét. Copyright 1933 by Rosemary and Stephen Vincent Benét. Copyright renewed 1961 by Rosemary Carr Benét. Reprinted by permission of Brandt & Brandt Literary Agents, Inc.

The Christian Science Monitor for "And Stands There Sighing" by Elizabeth Coatsworth. Copyright 1946 by The Christian Science Publishing Society. All rights reserved. Reprinted by permission of *The Christian Science Monitor.*

William Cole for "Back Yard, July Night" from *A Boy Named Mary Jane and Other Silly Verse* by William Cole (Franklin Watts, Inc., 1977). Copyright © 1969 by William Cole.

Philip Dacey for "Thumb" from *How I Escaped from the Labyrinth and Other Poems* by Philip Dacey (Carnegie-Mellon University Press, 1977).

Delacorte Press/Seymour Lawrence for "A Boat" and "Surprise" from *The Pill Versus the Springhill Mine Disaster* by Richard Brautigan. Copyright © 1968 by Richard Brautigan. For "There was an old lady named Crockett" from *Laughing Time* by William Jay Smith. Copyright 1953, © 1955, 1956, 1957, 1959, 1968, 1974, 1977, 1980 by William Jay Smith. All selections reprinted by permission of Delacorte Press/Seymour Lawrence.

Emanuel diPasquale for his poem "Rain," copyright © 1971, 1974, 1978, 1982 by Emanuel diPasquale.

Doubleday & Company, Inc. for "The Dancing Bear" from *Taxis and Toadstools* by Rachel Field. Copyright 1924 by Yale University Press. For "Night Journey" and "The Ceiling" (Copyright 1940, 1950 by Theodore Roethke) and "Child on Top of a Greenhouse" (Copyright 1946 by Editorial Publications, Inc.) from *The Collected Poems of Theodore Roethke.* All selections reprinted by permission of Doubleday & Company, Inc.

Dryad Press for "Saying Dante Aloud" from *Moments of the Italian Summer* by James Wright. Copyright © 1976 by James Wright. For "Zimmer in Grade School" from *The Zimmer Poems.* Copyright ©

1976 by Paul Zimmer, reprinted by permission of Paul Zimmer and Dryad Press.

The Estate of Norma Farber for "For a Quick Exit" by Norma Farber from *The New York Kid's Book*, edited by Catharine Edmonds *et al.* (Doubleday & Company, Inc.). Copyright © 1979 by Norma Farber.

Farrar, Straus & Giroux, Inc., for "stars" from *Spin a Soft Black Song* by Nikki Giovanni. Copyright © 1971, 1985 by Nikki Giovanni. Reprinted by permission of Hill and Wang, a division of Farrar, Straus & Giroux, Inc. For "Magnet" from *More Small Poems* by Valerie Worth. Copyright © 1976 by Valerie Worth. Reprinted by permission of Farrar, Straus & Giroux, Inc.

Ian Hamilton Finlay for "Great frog race" and "waterwheels in whirl" from *Poems to Hear and See* by Ian Hamilton Finlay (The Macmillan Company, 1971).

Walker Gibson for "Before Starting" from *Come As You Are* by Walker Gibson (Hastings House, 1958).

David R. Godine, Publisher, for "What Has Happened to Lulu?" from *Charles Causley 1951–1975, Collected Poems.* Copyright © 1975 by Charles Causley. Reprinted by permission of David R. Godine, Publisher, Inc., Boston.

Grosset & Dunlap, Inc. for "Football" from *Walt Mason, His Book* by Walt Mason. Copyright 1916 by Barse & Hopkins. Reprinted by permission of Grosset & Dunlap, Inc.

Donald Hall for "A Second Stanza for Dr. Johnson" from *Exiles and Marriages* by Donald Hall (The Viking Press, 1956). Copyright © 1956, 1984 by Donald Hall.

Harcourt Brace Jovanovich, Inc., for translations of "A bantam rooster" and "Small bird, forgive me" in *More Cricket Songs* by Harry Behn. Copyright © 1971 by Harry Behn. For "Splinter" from *Good Morning, America* by Carl Sandburg. Copyright 1928, © 1956 by Carl Sandburg. For "Listening to grownups quarreling" from *The Marriage Wig and Other Poems* by Ruth Whitman. Copyright © 1968 by Ruth Whitman. All selections reprinted by permission of Harcourt Brace Jovanovich, Inc.

Harper & Row, Inc., for "We Real Cool: The Pool Players. Seven at the Golden Shovel" from *The World of Gwendolyn Brooks.* Copyright © 1959 by Gwendolyn Brooks. For "Incident" from *On These I Stand* by Countee Cullen. Copyright 1925 by Harper & Row, Publishers, Inc., renewed 1953 by Ida M. Cullen. For "Snowy Benches" from *Out in the Dark and Daylight* by Aileen Fisher. Copyright © 1980 by Aileen Fisher. For "Knitted Things" from *Dogs and Dragons, Trees and Dreams* by Karla Kuskin. Copyright © 1964 by Karla Kuskin. For "The Child on the Shore" from *Hard Words and Other Poems* by Ursula K. LeGuin. Copyright © 1981 by Ursula K. LeGuin. For "One of the Years," copyright © 1975 by William Stafford and "A Story That Could be True," copyright © 1976 by William Stafford, both from *Stories That Could Be True* by William Stafford. For "Coming from the woods" and "The green cockleburs" from *Richard Wright Reader* edited by Ellen Wright and Michel Fabre. Copyright © 1978 by Ellen Wright and Michel Fabre. All selections reprinted by permission of Harper & Row, Publishers, Inc.

William J. Harris for his poem "An Historic Moment."

Harvard University Press for "A word is dead" from *The Poems of Emily Dickinson* edited by Thomas H. Johnson (Cambridge, Mass.): The Belknap Press of Harvard University Press). Copyright 1951,

Acknowledgments

© 1955, 1979, 1983 by the President and Fellows of Harvard College. Reprinted by permission of the publishers and the Trustees of Amherst College.

Ronald Hobbs Literary Agency for "Christmas morning i" by Carol Freeman.

Holt, Rinehart & Winston for "The Golf Links" from *Portraits and Protests* by Sarah N. Cleghorn. All rights reserved. For "Beyond Words" and "Canis Major" from *The Poetry of Robert Frost* edited by Edward Connery Lathem. Copyright 1928, 1947, © 1969 by Holt, Rinehart & Winston. Copyright © 1956 by Robert Frost. Copyright © 1975 by Lesley Frost Ballantine. For "Her strong enchantments failing" from *The Collected Poems of A. E. Housman*. Copyright 1922 by Holt, Rinehart & Winston. Copyright 1950 by Barclays Bank Ltd. All selections reprinted by permission of Holt, Rinehart & Winston, Publishers.

Houghton Mifflin Company for "On Learning to Adjust to Things" from *Fast and Slow* by John Ciardi. Copyright © 1975 by John Ciardi. For "Crying" from *Mortal Acts, Mortal Words* by Galway Kinnell. Copyright © 1980 by Galway Kinnell. For "Wind and Silver" from *The Complete Poetical Works of Amy Lowell*. Copyright © 1955 by Houghton Mifflin Company. For "The Riddle Song" from *The Ballad Book of John Jacob Niles*. Copyright © 1960, 1961 by John Jacob Niles. For "Science Fiction" from *The Mother's Breast and the Father's House* by Reed Whittemore. Copyright © 1974 by Reed Whittemore. All selections reprinted by permission of Houghton Mifflin Company.

The Hudson Review for "Spruce Woods" by A. R. Ammons in *The Hudson Review*, Vol. XXXIII, No. 1 (Spring 1980). Copyright © 1980 by A. R. Ammons.

Hutchinson Publishing Group Ltd. for "Childhood" from *Collected Poems* by Frances Cornford (Cresset Press). Reprinted by Permission of Hutchinson Publishing Group Ltd.

International Creative Management for "My Fingers" from *My Fingers Are Always Bringing Me News* by Mary O'Neill (Doubleday, 1969). Copyright © 1969 by Mary O'Neill. Reprinted by permission of International Creative Management, Inc.

Alfred A. Knopf, Inc., for "Winter Moon" from *Selected Poems of Langston Hughes*. Copyright 1926 by Alfred A. Knopf, Inc., renewed 1954 by Langston Hughes. For "September" from *A Child's Calendar* by John Updike, illustrated by Nancy Burkert. Copyright © 1965 by John Updike and Nancy Burkert. For "Winter Ocean" from *Telephone Poles and Other Poems* by John Updike. Copyright © 1960 by John Updike. All selections reprinted by permission of Alfred A. Knopf, Inc.

Kenneth Koch for "Variations on a Theme by William Carlos Williams" from *Thank You and Other Poems* by Kenneth Koch (Grove Press, 1962).

Ted Kooser for "Child Frightened by a Thunderstorm," "Country School," and "Genuine Poem, Found on a Blackboard in a Bowling Alley in Story City, Iowa" from *Official Entry Blank* by Ted Kooser (University of Nebraska Press, 1969).

Ray Lincoln Literary Agency for "The Hound" from *Don't Ever Cross a Crocodile and Other Poems* by Kaye Starbird. Copyright © 1963 by Kaye Starbird.

Little, Brown & Company for "Blesséd Lord, what it is to be young" from *One at a Time* by David McCord. Copyright © 1961 by David McCord. For "The Purist" from *Family Reunion* by Ogden Nash. Copyright 1935 by The Curtis Publishing Co. First appeared in the *Saturday Evening Post*. For "The Termite" from *Family Reunion* by Ogden Nash. Copyright 1942 by The Curtis Publishing Co. First appeared in the *Saturday Evening Post*. For "Requiem" ("There was a young belle of old Natchez") from *I'm a Stranger Here Myself* by Ogden Nash. Copyright 1938 by Ogden Nash. All selections by permission of Little, Brown & Company. For "Analysis of Baseball" from *New and Selected Things Taking Place*

by May Swenson. Copyright © 1971 by May Swenson. By permission of Little, Brown & Company in association with the Atlantic Monthly Press.

Liveright Publishing Corp. for "In Just-" from *Tulips & Chimneys* by E. E. Cummings. Copyright 1923, 1925, and renewed 1951, 1953 by E. E. Cummings. Copyright © 1973, 1976 by Nancy T. Andrews. Copyright © 1973, 1976 by George James Firmage. Reprinted by permission of Liveright Publishing Corporation.

Myra Cohn Livingston for "4-Way Stop" from *4-Way Stop and Other Poems*. Copyright © 1976 by Myra Cohn Livingston. Reprinted by permission of Marian Reiner for the author.

Alan Lomax for "The Big Rock Candy Mountains" from *The Folk Songs of North America* by Alan Lomax (Doubleday, 1960).

Lothrop, Lee & Shepard Books for "Rural Recreation" from *The Sidewalk Racer and Other Poems of Sports and Motion* by Lillian Morrison. Copyright © 1974 by Lillian Morrison. First appeared in *Counter/Measures*. For "The Sidewalk Racer" and "Surf" from *The Sidewalk Racer and Other Poems of Sports and Motion* by Lillian Morrison. Copyright © 1977 by Lillian Morrison. All selections reprinted by permission of Lothrop, Lee & Shepard Books (A Division of William Morrow & Company).

Ludlow Music, Inc. for words and music to "Turkey in the Corn" by Woody Guthrie. Copyright © 1960 by Ludlow Music, Inc., New York, NY. Used by permission.

Macmillan of Canada for "There Was a Man" from *Nicholas Knock and Other People* by Dennis Lee. Copyright © 1974 by Dennis Lee. Reprinted by permission of Macmillan of Canada, a division of Canada Publishing Corp.

Macmillan Publishing Co., Inc., for "The Bird of Night" from *The Bat-Poet* by Randall Jarrell. Copyright © 1963, 1964 by Macmillan Publishing Co., Inc. For "The Wind" from *Collected Poems* by James Stephens. Copyright 1915 by Macmillan Publishing Co., Inc., renewed 1943 by James Stephens. For "The Old Men Admiring Themselves in the Water" by William Butler Yeats from *The Poems of W. B. Yeats*, edited by Richard J. Finneran (New York: Macmillan, 1983). All selections reprinted by permission of Macmillan Publishing Co., Inc.

David McCord for "When I was christened" from "Perambulator Poems" in *And What's More* by David McCord (Coward McCann). Copyright 1941 by David McCord.

Eve Merriam for "Landscape" from *Finding a Poem* by Eve Merriam (New York: Atheneum). Copyright © 1970 by Eve Merriam. For "Sing a Song of Subways" from *The Inner City Mother Goose* by Eve Merriam (New York: Simon and Schuster). Copyright © 1969 by Eve Merriam. For "Windshield Wiper" from *Out Loud* by Eve Merriam (New York: Atheneum). Copyright © 1973 by Eve Merriam. For "Counting-Out Rhyme" from *Rainbow Writing* by Eve Merriam (New York: Atheneum, 1976). Copyright © 1976 by Eve Merriam. All selections reprinted by permission of the author.

Josephine Miles for quotation from "Sale" in *Poems 1930–1960* by Josephine Miles (Indiana University Press, 1960).

New Directions Publishing Corp. for "The Innocent" from "Here and Now" in *Collected Earlier Poems 1940–1960* by Denise Levertov. Copyright © 1957 by Denise Levertov. For "The Magical Mouse" from *The Collected Poems of Kenneth Patchen*. Copyright 1952 by Kenneth Patchen. For "Raccoon" from *Collected Shorter Poems* by Kenneth Rexroth. Copyright © 1956 by New Directions Publishing Corporation. For "About an excavation" and "The house-wreckers" from *By the Waters of Manhattan* by Charles Reznikoff. Copyright 1927, 1934 by Charles Reznikoff. For "After weeks of watching the roof leak" from "Hitch Haiku" in *The Back Country* by Gary Snyder. Copyright © 1968 by Gary Snyder. For "Poem" and "This Is Just to Say" from *Collected Earlier Poems* by William Carlos Williams. Copyright 1938 by New Directions Publishing Corporation. All selections reprinted by permission of New Directions Publishing Corporation.

Harold Ober Associates, Inc., for "Subway Rush Hour" from *Montage of a Dream Deferred* by Langston Hughes (Henry Holt, 1951). Copyright 1951 by Langston Hughes. Copyright renewed 1979 by George H. Bass for the Estate of Langston Hughes. Reprinted by permission of Harold Ober Associates, Inc.

Oxford University Press (U.K.) for "My Old Cat" from *Tomorrow Is My Love* by Hal Summers. Copyright © 1978 by Hal Summers. Reprinted by permission of Oxford University Press.

A. D. Peters & Co. Ltd. for "The Knowledgeable Child" from *Selected Poems* by L. A. G. Strong (William Collins Sons & Co. Ltd.). Reprinted by permission of A. D. Peters & Co. Ltd.

Laurence Pollinger Limited and the Estate of Frieda Lawrence Ravagli for "The White Horse" from *The Complete Poems of D. H. Lawrence* (London: William Heinemann Limited, 1967).

Dudley Randall for his poem "Blackberry Sweet."

Willie Reader for "When Paul Bunyan Was III" from *Back Packing* by Willie Reader (New Collage Press, 1975).

Paul R. Reynolds, Inc. for "Good Sportsmanship" from *Nights with Armour* by Richard Armour (McGraw-Hill, 1958). Used by permission.

Rev. Daniel J. Rogers for "child" by Raymond Roseliep. For "sky" from *A Roseliep Retrospective: Poems and Other Words By and About Raymond Roseliep* (Ithaca, New York: Alembic Press). Copyright © 1980 by Raymond Roseliep.

Louise H. Sclove for "Ancient History" from *Lyric Laughter* by Arthur Guiterman. Copyright 1939. Reprinted by permission of Louise H. Sclove.

Simon & Schuster for "In a cavern" from *Quake, Quake, Quake* by Paul Dehn. Copyright © 1958, 1961 by Paul Dehn. For "Yield" from *Pop Poems* by Ronald Gross. Copyright © 1967 by Ronald Gross. For "The Slithergadee" ("Not Me") from *Uncle Selby's Zoo — Don't Bump the Glump* by Shel Silverstein. Copyright © 1964 by Shel Silverstein. All selections reprinted by permission of Simon & Schuster, a Division of Gulf & Western Corp.

William Jay Smith for "Brooklyn Bridge" from *The New York Kid's Book* edited by Catharine Edmonds *et al.* (Doubleday & Company, 1979). Copyright © 1979 by Doubleday & Company. For "Said Dorothy Hughes to Helen Hocking" from *Mr. Smith and Other Nonsense* by William Jay Smith (Delacorte Press/Seymour Lawrence, 1969). Copyright © 1969 by William Jay Smith. Both selections reprinted by permission of William Jay Smith.

The Society of Authors for "Her strong enchantments failing" by A. E. Housman. Reprinted by permission of The Society of Authors as the literary representative of the Estate of A. E. Housman, and Jonathan Cape, Ltd., publisher of A. E. Housman's *Collected Poems*. For "The Wind" by James Stephens. Reprinted by permission of The Society of Authors on behalf of the copyright owner, Mrs. Iris Wise.

University of Illinois Press and Josephine Miles for "Travelers" from *Coming to Terms* by Josephine Miles (University of Illinois Press, 1979). Copyright © 1979 by Josephine Miles.

The University of Massachusetts Press for "While I Slept" from *Robert Francis: Collected Poems, 1936–1976* (The University of Massachusetts Press, 1976). Copyright 1936, © 1964 by Robert Francis.

Viking Penguin Inc. for "Do It Yourself" from *The Skin Spinners* by Joan Aiken. Copyright © 1975 by Joan Aiken. For "The White Horse" from *The Complete Poems of D. H. Lawrence* edited by Vivian de la Sola Pinto and Warren Roberts. Copyright © 1964, 1971 by Angelo Ravagli and C. M. Weekley, Executors of the Estate of Frieda Lawrence Ravagli. For "Triolet Against Sisters" from *Times Three* by Phyllis McGinley. Copyright © 1959 by Phyllis McGinley. Originally published in *The New Yorker*. For "Mr. Wells" from *Under the Tree* by Elizabeth Maddox Roberts. Copyright 1924 by B. W. Huebsch, Inc., renewed 1950 by Ivor S. Roberts. Copyright 1930, renewed 1958 by The Viking Press, Inc. All selections reprinted by permission of Viking Penguin Inc.

José Garcia Villa for "To Become an Archer" from *Selected Poems and New* by José Garcia Villa (McDowell, Obolensky, 1958). Copyright © 1958 by José Garcia Villa.

Anita Virgil for "grass path lasts" from *A 2nd Flake* by Anita Virgil. Copyright © 1974 by Anita Virgil.

Nick Virgilio for his poem "Now the swing is still." First appeared in *Haiku West Magazine*, Forest Hills, New York.

Warner Bros. Inc., for "Blowin' in the Wind" by Bob Dylan. Copyright © 1962 by Warner Bros. Inc. All rights reserved. Used by permission.

A. P. Watt Ltd. for "Hide and Seek" from *The Poor Boy Who Followed His Star and Children's Poems* by Robert Graves. By permission of A. P. Watt Ltd. and Robert Graves. For "The Old Men Admiring Themselves in the Water" from *Collected Poems* by William Butler Yeats. By permission of A. P. Watt Ltd., M. B. Yeats, Anne Yeats, and Macmillan London Limited.